I0428989

Free Will Baptist

Ministers

Buried

In

Oklahoma

Complied

By

Winnie Vance Yandell

Copyright 2016
By
Winnie Yandell

ISBN 978-1523836482 Soft cover

This book was printed in the United States of America.

To order additional copies of this book, contact:

Winnie Yandell
wmyan@sbcglobal.net
Or
www.amazon.com

FWB
FWB Publications
Enchanting Acres
1006 Rayme Drive
Columbus, Ohio 43207

Foreword

I've always thought ministers were worthy of honor and should be esteemed for 'works sake' if nothing else. Probably, this feeling was influenced by my early upbringing in the Free Will Baptist denomination in a country church which had deacons who "looked after" the church when no preacher was available. On many occasions I heard their testimonies about the beloved Rev. Henry "San" Huckeby, organizer of the church in 1908. I even wondered at that time, 'where did he go, and where did he die?' Later on, as I thought about it, I knew of no ready source to find him.

My late husband's father, Dr. I.W. Yandell, knew our church's history, doctrines and its progress, especially in Oklahoma where he had played a leading role. I know this influenced my husband's attention to the subject as well. I also listened to many interesting dialogues in our home when my husband and another minister, or missionary conversed, and I'm pretty sure as a consequence it had an effect on me as well.

After I retired, and America went 'on-line' I began to search names of the ministers I had known that had passed from earth to heaven---to find where they were buried. Did they die in California? Missouri? Arkansas? Texas? Or another state. It piqued my curiosity. Then, there were others I scarcely knew. Where were they?

Old Oklahoma Minutes were dusted off as I checked the "Ministers List." And, a name in a book could enlist hours of searching for his grave. Some, I paid small fees to some county/town libraries for a copy of an obituary or information they held. Oklahoma did not require death records before 1907, and mostly until about 1915, none were sent in. Many country cemeteries did not have a list of cemetery burials. I posted on county message boards online, and some responded by saying they were a descendant and gave me information, especially in those who died in the early years of our statehood. I'm sorry to say there are some I have not been able to locate at this time.

If the reader looks for a minister who lived and preached in Oklahoma, and you do not find him here, you will need to look in the more extensive work of ALL the states by Dr. Alton Loveless, who has published volumes with names listed by state where they are buried. Many Oklahoma ministers moved to other states where they died and were buried.

We're told that God has a "book of remembrance" and, my prayer is that we all will have our names in this most important Book.

--Winnie M. (Vance) Yandell

Acknowledgment

My gratitude cannot be fully expressed here to Dr. Alton E. Loveless, retired Free Will Baptist Publisher of Randall House Publications in Nashville, Tennessee, and many other estimable positions he has held during his fruitful ministry.

He has graciously offered without fee, his talents, time and efforts to bring this little book of Burials of our Free Will Baptist Ministers in OK. in print form for me.

He has compiled in several Volumes the names of FWB ministers buried all across our nation, Canada, and other lands where they have died.

He has done a great service for our denomination to preserve this valuable resource for us. I know, and hope the reader knows, what it means to have this written down for our posterity.

I could not have had this printed without his help. Saying 'thank-you' to him is not enough so I've asked the Giver of all good gifts, to repay him according to His unlimited riches in Glory.

I also appreciate all others who sent me information, obituaries, family history, etc., even some of the older ministers who died before statehood. Also, librarians, county clerks and cemetery sextons, were very helpful.

--Winnie M. Yandell

"The steps of a good man are ordered by the LORD: and he delighteth in his way. Though he fall, he shall not be utterly cast down: for the LORD upholdeth him with his hand. I have been young, and now am old; yet have I not seen the righteous forsaken, nor his seed begging bread... For the LORD loveth judgment, and forsaketh not his saints; they are preserved for ever: but the seed of the wicked shall be cut off... But the salvation of the righteous is of the LORD: he is their strength in the time of trouble,"

(Psalm 37:23-25, 28, 39).

Oklahoma

Eldie Clifton Able

Birth:
Aug. 28, 1937
Coweta,
Wagoner County, Oklahoma
Death:
Jan. 5, 2010
Tulsa,
Tulsa County, Oklahoma
Burial:
Vernon Cemetery, Coweta,
Wagoner County, Oklahoma

A retired machinist, Eldie was an active minister who enjoyed mowing, painting cement figurines, horses, reading Westerns and especially his grandchildren.

Maxi Lee Adair

Birth:
Jan. 10, 1940
El Paso, El Paso County, Texas
Death:
Aug. 6, 2012
Muskogee, Muskogee County,
Oklahoma
Burial:
Greenhill Cemetery Muskogee,
Muskogee County, Oklahoma

Maxi graduated from Tahlequah High School in 1959. In 1960, he joined the United States Army and received an honorable discharged in 1963. He worked for Acme Engineering beginning in 1965 until his retirement in 2002. Maxi gave his life to God on March 14, 1969 and surrendered to preach New Year's Eve 1974. He pastored the Grovania Free Will Baptist Church, Fort Gibson Free Will Baptist Church, Hitchita Free Will Baptist Church, and the First Free Will Baptist Church in Muskogee.

Rev Delbert Akin
Birth:
Nov. 22, 1927
Pottawatomie County
Oklahoma
Death:
Nov. 16, 2014
Midwest City
Oklahoma County
Oklahoma
Burial:
Resthaven Memorial Park
Shawnee
Pottawatomie County
Oklahoma

James Delbert Akin, 86, was born to Daniel and Anna Akin in Maud, OK.

He began this ministry at the First FWB church in Tecumseh, Ok on June 10, 1951. He has pastored the following FWB Churches all of which are in Oklahoma: Tecumseh Church, 1951-1956; Ada First, 1956-1963; Norman First, 1963-1967; Spencer Road, 1967-1968; Ada First, 1968-1977; Ardmore First, 1977-1980; Westgate, Shawnee, as a missionary for First OK Association 1980-1989; Tecumseh 1989-1991; Wolf Church 1991-1993; Choctaw 1993-2004; Senior Adult Pastor at Harrah FWB Church 2004 to his death.

Akin has been active in serving his denomination while serving as a Pastor. He was Oklahoma Executive Secretary 1953-1955 on a part-time basis, a member of the State Mission Board 1955-1975, member of the National Home Mission Board 1974-1985, and a member of the Hillsdale College Board of Trustees, 1975-1985. He was on the faculty of Hillsdale College for a number of years, 1965-1989, teaching English and Speech and was Director of the Ministerial Intern Program. He was a member of the Ministers Quartet for 43 years, and United Commercial Travelers 1960-present where he served as International Secretary Treasurer for a number of years.

His service was held at Hillsdale Free Will Baptist College in Moore.

Elder William Charles Austin
Birth:
Jun., 1864
Savannah,
Hardin County, Tennessee
Death:1933
Shawnee, Pottawatomie County,
Oklahoma
Burial:
Fairview Cemetery,
Shawnee, Pottawatomie County,
Oklahoma

He was an ordained Free Will Baptist preacher, but research is needed to obtain the date he was ordained. His name is in old church records as having preached several years before statehood in 1907. He was a prominent preacher and able debater in the central part of Oklahoma, and western Arkansas. He was an acceptable orator, and a great preacher. Many were converted under his ministry, and it is unknown just how many churches he organized, but he did a good work. He was editor of a church paper, *The Pruning Hook.*

Starks Washington Baldwin
Birth:
Jun. 23, 1865
Tawamba County, Mississippi
Death:
Jan. 27, 1920
Wister,Le Flore County,
Oklahoma
Burial:
Ellis Chapel Cemetery,
Wister,Le Flore County,
Oklahoma

Rev John Henry Ballard, Sr
Birth:
May 22, 1935
Stratford
Garvin County
Oklahoma
Death:
Jun. 24, 2013
Norman
Cleveland County
Oklahoma
Burial:
McGee Cemetery
Stratford
Garvin County
Oklahoma

John was born OK to Leslie and Lucy (Ernest) Ballard. He was raised and attended school in Stratford, graduating about 1953. John married Margaret Thompson on April 15, 1954 in Stratford. He continued his education at Hillsdale Freewill Baptist College in Moore. They made their home in the area in 1973. John was a minister and pastored many churches.

He was pastor and a member of the Lexington Free Will Baptist Church at the time of his death. He preached his last sermon a week or so before his death.

He enjoyed fishing, mowing, eating, attending and singing at revivals, and spending time with his family.

Jerry served as a missionary in Japan for 19 years and a pastor in Colquitt, Georgia, and Cushing, Oklahoma. He was also an instructor at Hillsdale FWB College as is his wife Dr. Janice Banks. He also was serving as pastor of Kingsview FWB Church, So. OKC, when he was tragically killed in an auto accident

Jerry Cleo Banks
Birth:
Aug. 3, 1948
Tulsa,
Tulsa County, Oklahoma
Death:
Jan. 6, 2005
Oklahoma
Burial:
Moore Cemetery, Moore,
Cleveland County
Oklahoma

Alford Barnhill
Birth:
Jan. 19, 1810
Tennessee
Death:
Mar. 3, 1899
Arpelar, Pittsburg County,
Oklahoma
Burial:
White Chimney Cemetery,
Stuart,
Pittsburg County Oklahoma

He was ordained as Free Will Baptist preacher, but unknown when and where. He came into Indian Territory, in what is now Oklahoma, where these pioneer ministers preached and organized churches for the settlers. When several churches were organized, they met at Nubbin Ridge school house, near Spiro, Choctaw Nation, Sept. 1, 1894, and formed the Territorial Association of Free Will Baptists. Eld. A. Barnhill, was elected the first moderator, Eld. O.J. Taylor, Ass't Moderator, and Eld. I.W. Graham, clerk. Eld. A. Barnhill's name appears in old Territorial marriage records of those he performed.

John Barnes
Birth:
Jul. 19, 1917
Cherokee County, Oklahoma
Death:
Dec. 3, 2014
Muskogee
Muskogee County, Oklahoma
Burial:
White Oak Cemetery
Qualls, Cherokee County
Oklahoma

John Barnes, 97, of Gore, was a Free Will Baptist minister per church records. And was bi-vocational working in construction.

Rev Pleasant A Barton, Jr
Birth:
Jan. 5, 1940
Sulphur, Oklahoma
Death:
Mar. 4, 2010
Burial:
Oaklawn Cemetery
Sulphur, Murray County,
Oklahoma

Rev. Pleasant A. Barton, Jr., our beloved Husband, Daddy and Papa passed away on Thursday, March 4, 2010, surrounded by his family as he crossed over into Heaven's Gates. He exemplified the true definition of a Champion and valiant warrior, as he fought Parkinson's disease for the last fifteen years of his life.

Junior was born to P. A. (Buck) Barton and Goldie Bulla Barton. He and his high school sweetheart, Lawana Sue Fisher, were married November 2, 1957, at Gainesville, Texas. Junior and Sue graduated from Sulphur High School in 1958. For over 24 years, he had been a faithful employee of the Oklahoma Vending Company. He had served in the Oklahoma National Guard and the 4002 Army Reserve Service Unit. The most important thing in his life was to know and serve his personal Savior, Jesus Christ. Of Free Will Baptist faith, he had served as pastor of several churches around the Ardmore area. Prior to recently moving to Ardmore.

Sunny Lane Cemetery, Del City, Oklahoma County, Oklahoma

He was an ordained Free Will Baptist minister. His brother, Will L. Bean, was also a preacher. In Oklahoma during the 1920's through 1950's. Rev. Bean was very active, and known as an outstanding evangelist. He was chosen to preach in the 1932 and 1934 Oklahoma FWB State Associations. He authored the book, *"What Would the World Be Without the Bible,"* a book that defends the Biblical record in various aspects of its historical statements. He is also author of a number of poems based on Bible subjects, and being a natural elocutionist, he often recited from memory upon request.

John E. Bean
Birth:
1876
Texas
Death:
May, 1961
Edmond,
Oklahoma County, Oklahoma
Burial:

Rev Leonard Bean
Birth:
1898
Death:
1996
Burial:
Wetumka Cemetery
Wetumka

Hughes County
Oklahoma

An ordained Free Will Bapt. minister and pastor. He pastored churches in Hughes County, and surrounding areas.

Eugene Benson
Birth:
Feb. 3, 1933
Death:
Aug. 27, 2004
Fort Smith
Sebastian County
Arkansas
Burial:
Howe Cemetery
Howe
Le Flore County
Oklahoma

Minister and pastor for many years. Korean War Navy Veteran.

Ransom "Rance" Bess
Birth:
Apr. 22, 1844
Grenada,
Grenada County, Mississippi
Death:
Aug. 5, 1932
Pontotoc County, Oklahoma

Burial:
Egypt Cemetery, Ada,
Pontotoc County, Oklahoma

Early pioneer minister of the Chickasaw Nation (Pontotoc Co. OK). He was well-liked and esteemed and ministered to many. Civil War Veteran Pvt. Co. F, 18th TX Ochiltree's Inf. CSA

Paskel Dale Bevan
Birth:
Apr. 15, 1946
Death:
Sep. 3, 2010
Burial:
Friends Church Cemetery,
Cromwell,
Seminole County Oklahoma

Paskel was the owner and operator of Seminole Sheet Metal for many years. He was also a longtime minister of the Friends Free Will Baptist Church of Seminole County. Paskel also enjoyed reading his Bible and helping build missionary churches.

Rev Roy Melvin Bingham

Birth:
Dec. 21, 1900
Drynob
Laclede County, Missouri
Death:
Nov. 15, 1971
Tulsa
Tulsa County, Oklahoma
Burial:
Rose Hill Memorial Park , Tulsa
Tulsa County, Oklahoma
Plot: Section Memories (16) L-678
#3

He was the son of William and Clara Bell (Ferguson) BINGHAM and married Opal Gregory, on Sept. 16, 1917, in Laclede Co. MO. He and his wife had three children.

His family was in Missouri in the 1920 census, but before 1930, they had moved to the Tulsa area, he as a bi-vocational minister, and was working as a "steel worker" to support his family.

Family history reports he began preaching at age 16; after he moved to Oklahoma, he pastored churches, held revivals, and was established by reputation and work, so that they sent him as a delegate from the Cooperative Association of Free Will Baptist from OK, to the organizational meeting of the National Association of the FWB, at Cofer's Chapel Church, Nashville, TN. in 1935.

He was active, productive, and was loved and respected among his brethren.

W. M. Bingham

Birth:
Feb. 26, 1871
Death:
Mar. 11, 1947
Burial:
Sub-Station Cemetery,
Freedom Hill,
Creek County, Oklahoma

Kenneth Brandon

Birth:
Sep. 6, 1921,
Death:
Jan. 29, 2008
Talihina, Le Flore County,
Oklahoma
Burial:
Macedonia Cemetery,
Pocola,
Le Flore County, Oklahoma

Rev. Brandon was a veteran of World War II, where he served in the Marine Corps, receiving a

Purple Heart for wounds received during the Bougainville Island campaign. He started and pastored many Freewill Baptist Churches in his lifetime. He never had much in the way of material wealth; he gave everything he had to the less fortunate.

Rev Joe Blair
Birth:
Nov. 26, 1934
Purcell
McClain County, Oklahoma
Death:
Jul. 25, 1998
Oklahoma City
Oklahoma County
Oklahoma
Burial:
Willow View Cemetery
Cleveland County, Oklahoma

The Rev. Joe Blair answered the call to preach at age fifteen, and began pastoring at age sixteen. He invested 50 years of ministry in Okla. and Calif. Free Will Baptist churches. He organized one church in Calif. and pastored four. He pastored seven OK churches. His final pastorate at Southwest FWB Church, OK, lasted 20 yrs.

The congregation voted him Pastor Emeritus title. The church had planned an Aug. 30th celebration to honor his 50 years in the ministry.

Joe stayed active in district, state, and national works. He served 16 yrs. as moderator of Oklahoma District First Oklahoma Association.

Funeral services were conducted by Revs. Wade T. Jernigan, and Jack Richey.

William "Bill" Bratcher
Birth:
Oct. 16, 1916
Garvin County, Oklahoma
Death:
Mar. 31, 2012
Oklahoma
Burial:
McGee Cemetery, Stratford,
Garvin County, Oklahoma

The Ada Newspaper: April 3, 2012 Stratford —Mr. Bratcher was ordained in the Free Will Baptist church in the late 1940's, in Pontotoc Co. OK. He preached and ministered to churches throughout the area.

Ernest E. Bristow
Birth:
Aug. 31, 1894
Tecumseh,
Pottawatomie County, Oklahoma
Death:
Nov. 26, 1941
Asher, Pottawatomie County,
Oklahoma
Burial:
Wanette Cemetery, Wanette,
Pottawatomie County, Oklahoma

After he finished college, he taught school in many small oil towns in south central Okla. He was also an ordained minister, and music instructor, and often led the singing in many churches. He taught "singing schools" in communities all over that area. Related to teaching school, his name is found in the old 1920's Ada Weekly newspaper with items such as, "E.E. Bristow, Stratford, teacher, for 8 terms; then "Prof. Bristow with his able corps of teachers attended teachers meeting Thursday, Friday and Saturday." He had left Oklahoma to find work in California due to hardships following dustbowl. He worked one day there, had a heart attack and returned to Oklahoma where he died a few months later.

In the book, *"History of Oklahoma Free Will Baptist State Association, 100 Years, 1908-2008"*, pub. 2008, it records that in 1926, "Eld. E. E. Bristow, was Rep. from Center to the State Ass'n of FWB, and in the 1932 annual state Association, he was elected clerk of that organization.

You Are Home At Last!

Rev Joseph H. Brown
Birth:
1853
Illinois
Death:
1924
Burial:
Fairlawn Cemetery
Oklahoma City
Oklahoma County
Oklahoma

Rev. J.H. Brown, is named in an early list of ministers, who was in the early organization of the Territorial Association of Free Will Baptist churches, in 1894, near Spiro, OK."

Rev Connie Dearl Cariker
Birth:
Nov. 15, 1935
Hoyt
Haskell County, Oklahoma
Death:
Feb. 21, 2016
Jenks
Tulsa County, Oklahoma
Burial:
Hoyt Cemetery
Hoyt
Haskell County, Oklahoma

Connie Dearl Cariker passed from this life on February 21, 2016, at his home in Jenks, Oklahoma. Connie Was born, the third of sixteen children, to Champ Clark Cariker and Joy Myree (Cleveland) Cariker at Hoyt, Oklahoma. He grew up in the Hoyt area and attended school at Hoyt School, Stigler High School, and Oklahoma Bible College.

Connie married Wanda Glo Gideon, on November 2, 1954, in Hoyt, Oklahoma. They moved to West Texas, where he worked in the West Texas Oil Fields. Upon moving to Tulsa, Oklahoma in 1956, He worked at Sunray DX Refinery. During his time at DX, Connie answered God's Call to preach. Soon after, in January of 1962, he became the full time pastor of the West Tulsa Free Will Baptist Church. He remained at the church as pastor for 21 years, during which time he served on the National Free Will Baptist Sunday School Board. In February of 1983, Connie took a position with the National Home Mission Department of the National Association of Free Will Baptists in Nashville, Tennessee, where he pioneered church growth and evangelism programs, and conducted church growth and evangelism conferences across the U.S. In January of 1986 Connie took the position of Executive Director of Oklahoma Free Will Baptists in Moore, Oklahoma. He left this position in 1994 to return to the pastorate of West Tulsa Free Will Baptist Church. He pastored there until his retirement from full time ministry in January, 2004. During his early retirement he remained active in ministry by preaching many revival services across the denomination.

Connie was an avid sports fan, especially of the St. Louis Cardinals. He loved people and loved to share the Gospel of Jesus Christ. He was an encourager to all and loved by many.

Services were at West Tulsa Free Will Baptist Church, 930 W. 23rd Pl., Tulsa, OK. Rev. Russell Payne and Rev. Dennis Cariker will be officiating.

Edna Hunt Buckelew
Birth:
1909
Death:
1985
Burial:
McGee Cemetery,
Stratford,
Garvin County, Oklahoma
She was a Free Will Baptist minister in the early part of Center Association, OK.

Robert William Carter
Birth:
Apr. 30, 1916
Ola, Yell County, Arkansas
Death:
Sep. 5, 2001

Broken Arrow,
Tulsa County, Oklahoma
Burial:
Park Grove Cemetery,
Broken Arrow,
Tulsa County, Oklahoma
A Free Will Baptist minister, Rev. Carter was licensed in 1957 and ordained in 1958. He pastored churches in California, Arkansas, Missouri and Oklahoma.

James Nathaniel Caton
Birth:
Oct. 14, 1862
Cooper County, Missouri
Death:
May 18, 1953
Ada, Pontotoc County, Oklahoma
Burial:
Oakman Cemetery,
Oakman,
Pontotoc County, Oklahoma

Old Brother" Caton, as he is known to his innumerable friends, was born in Missouri where he grew to young manhood, and remembered back as he tells of the time when the "Bluecoats," part of Custer's army, passed through his town on their way to the badlands of South Dakota. He left his home state of Missouri in 1886 for Texas. He was a farmer, made a few crops in Texas, moved to Oakland, Indian Territory, and made a crop, then back to Texas and in 1895, he moved to a place near Allen and lived in Pontotoc County. Definitely an Ada pioneer. Rev. Caton, a Free Will Baptist preacher since 1902, has probably married and buried as many people in the county as any other preacher. Even at 85, he still performed these ministerial duties. He has pastored at nearly every small community in the northern part of the county. His first pastorate was at Sikes school, where Atwood now stands. Other places where he pastored are Black Rock, Happyland, Cedar Grove, Yeager, Center, Culley west of Sasakwa, Pecan Grove, Stedman, McCalls Chapel, and Big Springs south of Wewoka. He was pastor of the Oakman church, his home community, for 19 years. At age 84, he was recalled as pastor with an assistant to take his place if he was unable to appear. Preaching in the "good old way," Caton would have four or five churches at the same time preaching in them only about once a month. He would arrive on Saturday in the community where he was pastor and hold one service that day, another on Sunday morning, another Sunday evening. During the summer session, he would hold revival meetings from two to five weeks long in each community he pastored.

Marion L. Caton
Birth:
Aug. 12, 1898
Pontotoc County, Oklahoma
Death:
Sep., 1965
Oklahoma City,
Oklahoma County, Oklahoma
Burial:
Arlington Memory Gardens,
Oklahoma City,
Oklahoma County, Oklahoma

He grew up around Oakman, Pontotoc Co. Oklahoma attending schools there. He was an ordained Free Will Baptist minister and pastor.

James Cearley
Birth:
Jul. 26, 1921
Death:
Sep. 19, 1996
Burial:
Tecumseh Cemetery, Tecumseh,
Pottawatomie County Oklahoma

He was a Free Will Baptist minister and a member of the US Navy during WW II.

James B. Chism
Birth:
May 12, 1925
Tupelo, Mississippi
Death:
Sep. 9, 2007
Tulsa, Oklahoma
Burial:
Floral Haven Memorial Gardens,
Broken Arrow,
Tulsa County, Oklahoma,
Plot: Sermon on the Mount
Garden

He grew up in East Tupelo where he played football and the clarinet in the band. After graduation he became a medic in the United States Army during World War II. After his discharge he married Imogene Martin on October 15, 1946. They both graduated from Bob Jones University in Greenville, S. C. where he earned a Master's Degree in Church History in 1952. He became the Minister of the Horse Branch Free Will Baptist Church in Turbeville, South Carolina. Later the First Free Will Baptist Church in Newport News, Virginia. In 1967 he moved his family to Tulsa to become the pastor of the New Home Free Will Baptist Church where he was

pastor until 1988 where he retired. He founded the greater Tulsa the seniors organization OASIS and was very active on the Oklahoma State Mission Board starting churches across the state. They served over six decades in the ministry.

Claude C. Chisum
Birth:
Mar. 25, 1894
Texas
Death:
Jun. 6, 1962
Hughes County, Oklahoma
Burial:
Non Cemetery,
Non, Hughes County,
Oklahoma

He served in the Infantry WW I, where he was exposed to mustard gas which caused him health problems thereafter. He lived in the Non community where he served the FWB church as a deacon for many years. He then was ordained as a minister of the gospel and pastored churches in the area, among them; Crossroads,

Calvin, and others, and preached wherever he was needed. He attended the Quarterly and State Association meetings.

Live For Eternity

William M. Coggins
Birth:
April 27, 1848
Texas
Death:
1946
Oklahoma
Burial:
McGee Cemetery, Stratford, Garvin County, Oklahoma

W. M. Coggins came to Indian Territory, probably after 1900, from Wise Co. Texas, upon request by a letter from Eld. Tom J. Townsend, an early arriver to the Indian Territory, asking him to come and help form some four churches into an association and preach for them. By 1904, he was preaching in the area churches from which the Center Association was formed in 1893 of Chickasaw Nation. He was elected to be moderator of this Center Association in 1906, following Rev. Mark Harris's move to Arkansas. He continued in this position for years, in most every session until his late retirement. He was pastor of several churches throughout the years, that included Blanchard in McClain Co., and his name appears in many old church records as having preached or pastored there. He was the elected delegate by this group to represent them in the Southwestern Association of Free Will Baptists, which met Nov. 1906 at Decatur, Texas. He was always in the forefront of leadership in the support of the Tecumseh FWB College which had been started in 1917. At the August 1946 session, it was reported that "our old beloved moderator has passed away;" then it was voted "for the Association to place a monument at his grave."

The Day Is Coming When All Will Hear His Voice.

Albert Lee Collier
Birth:
Jul. 25, 1918
Death:
Mar. 19, 2008
Burial:
Highland Cemetery,
Okemah,
Okfuskee County,
Oklahoma

He spent the majority of his life in and around the Okemah area. At the time of his death Albert was a member of the Okemah Free Will Baptist Church. He was ordained as a deacon in the Schoolton Free Will Baptist Church west of Okemah, April 10, 1949, and was ordained as a Free Will Baptist minister on May 20, 1951. He received a certificate of award from the Oklahoma Bible College on May 15, 1961. He helped organize Schoolton Free Will Baptist Church. He preached his second sermon after the organization of the church that Saturday on Schoolton corner. He preached his third sermon at Pleasant Oak School. His first pastorate was at the Schoolton Free Will Baptist Church. He also pastored Free Will Baptist Churches at Hannah, Sunnylane in Del City, Wewoka, Prague, Henryetta, Calvin, and Faith Free Will Baptist Church in Holdenville. He built or remodeled every place he pastored. He built an educational wing a new sanctuary at Sunnylane, a completely new facility at Wewoka, remodeled the facility at Prague and totally remodeled the Henryetta church. Brother Collier was instrumental in founding of the Okemah Free Will Baptist Church and labored in the construction of the facility under the pastorate of Brother Frank Young. The north wing of the church was dedicated in his honor. He served on the Oklahoma State Church Training Board, Oklahoma State Mission Board, and moderator of many associations while serving on several district boards. He celebrated 50 years of ministry on December 30, 2001. Records show that during his ministry he preached 170 funerals, 24 weddings, 56 revivals.

Leonard Crowder
Birth:
Apr. 12, 1917
Death:
Nov. 19, 2009
Barling,
Sebastian County,
Arkansas,
Burial:
Stigler Cemetery,
Stigler, Haskell County,
Oklahoma,

He was a Free Will Baptist Minister and a member of the Bethlehem Free Will Baptist Church of Van Buren, Arkansas.. He served in many churches in the area over the years but served as Pastor of the Walnut Street Free Will Baptist Church for over 30 years. He served in the Civil Conservation Corp and was an active member of the Ministerial Alliance of Fort Smith for many years.

Marvin P Dalton
Birth:
Mar. 9, 1906
Arkansas
Death:
Nov. 28, 1987
Tulsa County, Oklahoma
Burial:
Floral Haven Memorial Gardens,
Broken Arrow,
Tulsa County, Oklahoma

Well-known gospel song writer who was the son of William Henry Dalton and Effie (Thomas) Dalton.

who were both Free Will Baptist preachers in Arkansas and Oklahoma. Marvin, a noted and published song writer, with *"Looking for a City", "When Jesus Passed By",* and *"O' What a Saviour"* being the most popular of his songs. He attend Free Will Baptist Bible College in the late 40's. He directed music at the First Free Will Baptist Church in Tulsa under John West, but at the time of his passing was a member of the Assembly of God which had been the denomination of his wife.

Stephen Andrew Dame
Birth:
Feb. 9, 1847
Jasper, Marion County, Tennessee
Death
Apr. 3, 1927
Burial:
Center Cemetery, Center, Pontotoc County, Oklahoma, Plot: Dame Family (near entrance)

As a young boy, Stephen brought food and supplies to his older brother who was fighting in the Civil War. They moved from Jasper to Randolph County, Arkansas, in about 1878 or 1880. They lived in a tiny community known both as Water Valley and DeMun. Here, they built a log cabin. and farmed in Randolph County. Stephen was called to preach the Gospel at a young age. He could not read or write, but his wife could. She would read him passages from the Bible and he learned to read it. The Bible was the only thing he ever learned to read. He was a Freewill Baptist preacher. A man of great stature, Stephen stood 6'4" and was very slim. The obituary in the Ada Evening News (Ada, OK), read:"Rev. S. A. Dame, aged 82, died Sunday at 1 o'clock at his home at Center. Funeral services were set for this afternoon. Internment in Center cemetery. "Mr. Dame was a pioneer Freewill Baptist minister who had spent many years of his life in this country, doing his part in reclaiming it and making it a better place for later comers. He was highly respected by all who knew him."

William David "Voss" Dame
Birth:
Dec. 31, 1881
Death:
Jul. 23, 1957
Burial:
Center Cemetery, Center, Pontotoc County, Oklahoma

George S Davidson
Birth:
Jan. 17, 1890
Sunset, Texas
Death:
Oct. 4, 1966
Muskogee, Ok
Burial:
Greenlawn Cemetery
Checotah
McIntosh County
Oklahoma

Davidson was a veteran of World War One and a retired Free Will Baptist minister and U.S. Naval Ammunition Depot employee at McAlester. Funeral services with Rev. McCage officiating.

William Edward Dearmore
Birth:
May 25, 1881
Charleston, Arkansas
Death:
Dec. 12, 1945
Wanette,
Pottawatomie County, Oklahoma
Burial:
Wanette Cemetery, Wanette,
Pottawatomie County, Oklahoma

Rev. William Edward Dearmore was active in the first session of the Texas State Association of Free Will Baptists, which met at Bradley, Texas, October 8-9, 1915. We glean from the minutes of that meeting, written in Dearmore's own beautiful handwriting, several pieces of information about him. He was chosen to preach the "introductory sermon" at the meeting. The introductory sermon was the initial sermon preached at meetings in those days. They were what we today might call a keynote sermon or keynote address. This was a very distinct honor and indicates something of the high esteem in which Dearmore was held by his fellow Texas ministers. He was until the association could be organized, and then was elected permanent clerk. In addition, he was elected treasurer. Furthermore, he was appointed to serve with J. J. Tatum and C. C. Wheeler on a committee to draft a constitution for the fledgling association.

With numerous other ministers present, and with him being

appointed and/or elected to so many positions of great responsibility at the first session of the association, we learn something of the abilities with which he was gifted. At the time Dearmore lived in Boyd, Texas. Boyd is on State Highway 114 seven miles south of Decatur in southern Wise County.

At the second session of the Texas State Association, held in January of 1917, Dearmore was not present. He had made, or was preparing to make, a move to Oklahoma to be involved in the first year of operation of Tecumseh College. It seems that he took on more and larger responsibilities of ministry in Oklahoma. In addition to his years of service to Tecumseh College, where he served on the teaching faculty, he served a number of churches as pastor in Oklahoma, such as the Box Church and the Wolf Church. He served as moderator of the Oklahoma State Association a number of years: 1932, 1936-1939. He was also the owner of an insurance agency.

In 1935 he served as a delegate to the organizational meeting of the National Association of Free Will Baptists in Nashville, Tennessee. He was active in several sessions of the National Association thereafter. The Oklahoma State Association paid tribute to him in 1945 as a pioneer Free Will Baptist minister.

He was married to Ada Ann Baze on December 28, 1900, and they had seven children: William Henry (April 21, 1902 - April 29, 1909;

Ethel Idel (October 30, 1903 - July 2, 2975; Grace Lilly, January 11, 1910-December 6, 1992; James, August 30, 1914 - September 26, 1914; Floydette E. April 3, 1917 - September 26, 2002; Joy Yvonne, August 9, 1921 - January 1985; and Mildred Marie, July 4, 1923 - August 15, 1925).

His wife Ada was a teacher at Tecumseh College and served briefly as president of the school. She died on November 23, 1936, in Wanette. His World War II draft registration lists his wife as Mrs. Nora Dearmore. Apparently he had remarried after the death of Ada. His tombstone indicates that he was a Mason.

Austin R. Deaton, Sr
Birth:
Sep. 1, 1903
Death:
Sep. 17, 1967
Burial:
Rosedale Cemetery
Ada
Pontotoc County
Oklahoma, USA
Plot: N-112-7-4

Othel Thomas Dixon
Birth:
Jun. 20, 1919
Hector, Pope County, Arkansas
Death:
Oct. 27, 2007
Claremore,
Rogers County, Oklahoma
Burial:
Greenlawn Cemetery, Checotah,
McIntosh County, Oklahoma

He was the first Dixon to achieve outstanding All Star Basketball Player status. He graduated from Checotah High School in 1940. He moved to Oklahoma City working as a clerk at the Veterans Administration.

O.T. moved to Enid where he went to work at Vance Air Force Base as Personnel Director for the Army Air Corp. He was discharged from the Army Air Corp. in San Antonio, Texas.

They moved to Arkansas where he attended John Brown University and then College of the Ozarks where he obtained a degree in Education in 1952.

He pastored several Free Will Baptist Churches and built new buildings for the churches. He was ordained in May 1948 having served as pastor and evangelist for 59 years. Throughout his preaching career, he held many revivals throughout the United States. In the 1950's he published a book of sermons called, *Meetin' Time In The Ozarks*. He began a radio ministry while pastoring churches in Arkansas and Missouri. New buildings of worship were built during his pastorate at Charleston and Russellville, Arkansas, Mountain Grove and Springfield Missouri, and Norman, Oklahoma. In the late 1960's he obtained a Masters Degree in Counseling from Oklahoma City University. In 1976 he became the chaplain of the Oklahoma City Dept. of Corrections where he developed the Chaplaincy Program. He was a son of Rev. Thomas H. Dixon.

Thomas H Dixon
Birth:
Jun. 21, 1887
Hector,
Pope County, Arkansas

Death:
Feb. 14, 1973
Muskogee,
Muskogee County,
Oklahoma
Burial:
Greenlawn Cemetery,
Checotah,
McIntosh County, Oklahoma

A prominent Free Will Baptist preacher and church organizer, During his long tenure as pastor, Rev Dixon established several Free Will Baptist churches. He organized the Hitchita Free Will Baptist church in 1932 and served as pastor until 1937. In 1939 he organized the First Free Will Baptist Church in Checotah and served as pastor 11 years. He organized the Harmony Free Will Baptist Church at Hilltop and was its pastor at the time of his death. He pastored churches in both Arkansas and Oklahoma and served as state moderator for both Arkansas and Oklahoma.

Jerry D. Dudley
Birth:
Oct. 2, 1927
Oklahoma
Death:
Jan. 2, 1988
Garvin County,
Oklahoma
Burial:
McGee Cemetery,
Stratford,
Garvin County,
Oklahoma

Jerry was a WW II Navy veteran. He was raised by pious parents and early in life he became a Christian, and then entered the ministry. He entered ministerial studies at Nashville, Tennessee at Free Will Baptist Bible College in the late 1940's/1950's. His parents moved to California and Jerry and Bea began a pastorate at First FWB Church in Bakersfield, California. He pastored Tulare, CA where he saw the church grow and add members. He started a church in Oregon, and later was elected as Exec. Secretary of California FWB, where he helped edit *"The Voice"* the state paper. He accepted a pastorate in Oklahoma City, at Southern Oaks, where he built an additional facility. After several years, he entered the pastorate in Stratford FWB Church and at Choctaw. He was always active in his denomination's work, holding positions in the district, as well as state and national. Sadly, one daughter, Kaye, and her husband, John, who were on their itinerary for a mission assignment to Brazil, were killed in a tragic auto accident.

book, "History of Free Will Baptist," pub. 1958, that "at 7 o'clock, Rev. I.W. Yandell and Rev. D.B. Duniphin, preached uplifting discourses..."

Lewis Allen Edwards
Birth:
Dec. 11, 1842
Quincy
Adams County
Illinois
Death:
Jun. 20, 1918
Skiatook
Osage County
Oklahoma
Burial:
Ridgelawn Cemetery
Collinsville
Tulsa County
Oklahoma

D. B. Duniphin
Birth:
Feb. 22, 1858
Arkansas
Death:
Aug. 8, 1927
McClain County,
Oklahoma
Burial:
Fairview Cemetery
Tuttle, Grady County,
Oklahoma
Plot: Blk D, Lot 117

His parents were Burrel S. Duniphin and Nancy Jane "Annie" Gilmore. He married 1st: Mary Elizabeth STOVER, and they had several children. She died in 1900, and he married, 2) Mrs. Nannie J. Welsh Aug. 29, 1900, in Garvin Co. OK (from Kinard Files, on Indian Terr. marriages, Garvin Co, OK).When he entered the ministry is not known; but there is a record of The Southwestern Convention meeting at Tecumseh College, Dec. 26-30, 1917, recorded in G.W. Million's

Lewis enlisted in the Kansas 10th Volunteer Infantry Company "E" on July 23, 1861 and received an honorable discharged Aug 18, 1864. He married Nancy Jane Fredrick in Bourbon Co., KS on Apr 27, 1865. He moved his family to Elkins, AR in 1895 and in 1909 they came by covered wagons and settled in Skiatook, OK. (Info taken from book titled: Gateway to the Osage Nation)

Rev. Lewis A. Edwards. He consecrated his life to God in 1867; in 1878 he received license and Aug. 18, 1884, he was ordained in Pleasant Valley, Greenwood, KS. He has had pastoral charge of three churches, and been blessed of the Lord in his ministerial labors. He has served as clerk of the Row Valley Quarterly Meeting (QM) (KS) and the Kansas Southern Yearly Meeting.

Rev Arlie Barton Epperson
Birth:
Jul. 26, 1878
Bradley County
Tennessee
Death:
May 30, 1963
Burial:
Tecumseh Cemetery
Tecumseh
Pottawatomie County
Oklahoma

His parents were Thomas and Barthola Epperson, born Tenn. They removed to Oklahoma to the Shawnee and Tecumseh areas where they farmed. Arley Barton Epperson married Mattie Elizabeth Collins. He registered for both WW I and WW II Wars.

He was a minister, and was active in the Free Will Baptist church. Also, when the Tecumseh College was established by the Free Will Baptists, he was part of the faculty. In 1920, he and his wife lived in the Seminole area where they appeared in the census:

Cecil R. Fassio
Birth:
Jan. 18, 1927
Wilburton,
Latimer County, Oklahoma
Death:
Dec. 6, 2008
Hartshorne,
Pittsburg County, Oklahoma
Burial:
Springhill Cemetery,
Le Flore County, Oklahoma

He began his ministry in the 1950's and later became a Free Will Baptist ordained minister in 1966. He pastored various churches in Oklahoma and at Bell Gardens, California and in 1972 returned to Oklahoma to the Wilburton Free Will Baptist Church. He later made home in Stonewall, where he pastored the FWB church from 1979 to 1983. He moved to Hartshorne and be began pastoring the Hartshorne FWB Church until 1994, and later the Pittsburg FWB until 2001.They owned and operated the Little Rascals Day Care for more than 23 years.

Ward W Fellabaum
Birth:
Jun. 21, 1916
Death:
Feb. 21, 2001
Burial:
Tamaha Cemetery
Tamaha,
Haskell County,
Oklahoma

James Anderson Fergueson
Birth:
May 15, 1916
Olney, Texas
Death:
Mar. 28, 2011
Ardmore,
Carter County, Oklahoma
Burial:
Hall Cemetery,
Antlers,
Pushmataha County,
Oklahoma

Fergueson, known as J. A., died at the age of 94. J.A. married Velma Ella Ford on December 28, 1940, in Stephenville, Texas. He lived in this area since 1962, was a rancher, and raised dairy and beef cattle. J. A. also enjoyed hunting coyotes and wolves. He served his country as an artillery soldier in World War II, where he shot the big guns. He was a Free Will Baptist preacher and pastored the Mt. Zion, Pleasant View, Hall and the Free Will Baptist Church of Antlers.

William G Fields
Birth:
May 2, 1870
Cedar County, Missouri
Death:
Nov. 25, 1943
Seminole,
Seminole County, Oklahoma
Burial:
Tecumseh Cemetery, Tecumseh,
Pottawatomie County,
Oklahoma,
Plot: A2B8-R12-20

Rev. Fields was listed as an ordained Free Will Baptist minister in the Roll of Ministers in the old Center Association (Pontotoc Co) Minutes, as early as 1915, pastoring a church at Woodland. His name appears frequently in their records after 1917, preaching, pastoring and serving on boards and committees. In the 1919 Minutes, this is recorded, "Rev. W.G. Fields was elected delegate to the Co-Operative General Association which meets at Nashville, Tennessee." In his ministerial report of 1924, "travelled 1,430 miles; preached 106 sermons; conversions witnessed: 100; baptized 9; married two couples; conducted two funerals; receipts, $170.00."

He was living at Wanette, Pottawatomie, Oklahoma in the 1930 census and gave his occupation as teaching. He also pastored a church at Trousdale.

Sadie E Fincher
Birth:
Jul. 10, 1894
Indian Territory, Oklahoma.
Death:
Apr. 18, 1987
Burial:
Fairlawn Cemetery
Cushing
Payne County
Oklahoma,
Plot: Blk 10

Rev. Sadie Fincher, a pastor of the Olive Free Will Baptist Church and Silver City Free Will Baptist Church, She was 92 and born in Indian Territory, Oklahoma.

Jesse Augustus Fox
Birth:
May, 1861
Pike County, Arkansas
Death:
Aug. 8, 1932
Asher, Pottawatomie County, Oklahoma
Burial:
Vista Cemetery,
Asher, Pottawatomie County, Oklahoma

Between1910-1920, he came to Antlers, Pushmataha Co., Oklahoma where he and his wife, Savanna, were enumerated in 1920. In the southeastern Oklahoma marriage records, at Darwin, his name was listed as a "Free Will Baptist minister" who performed marriages there. Nothing is known where he was ordained, or of his ministerial labors.

Let other's seek a home below,
Which flames devour,
or waves o'er flow
Be mine a happier lot to own
A mansion in glory,
my own new home.

James Albert Franklin
Birth:
Sep. 29, 1910
Crawford County,
Arkansas
Death:
Aug. 23, 2003
Ada, Pontotoc County,
Oklahoma
Burial:
Fairlawn Cemetery,
Cushing,
Payne County, Oklahoma,
Plot: Blk 9

Rev. Franklin was an ordained minister of the Free Will Baptist Church for well over 60 years, pastoring churches in Arkansas, Oklahoma, and California. He was still active up until his death, supplying pulpits for pastors as needed.

Claud Freeman, Jr
Birth:
Oct. 10, 1926
Stratford, Garvin County,
Oklahoma
Death:
Aug. 2, 198 6
Ada, Pontotoc County, Oklahoma
Burial:
McGee Cemetery,
Stratford, Garvin County
Oklahoma

As a bi-vocational minister, he had pastored many area churches. He had retired from the Stratford Fire Department. He married Bernadean Ballard on Jun 15, 1945 in Stratford.

Howard Joe Gage
Birth:
Aug. 24, 1914
Death:
Aug. 24, 2005
Oklahoma
Burial:
Graham Memorial Cemetery,
Pryor,
Mayes County, Oklahoma

An ordained Free Will Baptist minister, pastor, missionary, and evangelist. Country Missionary Work and taking the Good News here and to different Countries.

As a missionary he served some time as a builder in the Ivory Coast, West Africa. He was also a member of the arm services achieving the rank of T Sgt U S Army World War Ii.

Jake W. Gage
Birth:
Feb. 5, 1891
Madison County, Arkansas
Death:
Mar., 1984
Pryor,
Mayes County, Oklahoma
Burial:
Fairview Cemetery, Pryor,
Mayes County, Oklahoma

In 1932, Jake was visiting an old-time preacher, Rev. George Washington Benton, on his farm, and was led to become a Christian. He began at once to witness to his friends, not intending to become a minister, but when a dear friend, Bob McClendon, died whom he had led to Christ, he was asked to preach his funeral. Jake's first revival was at the Paris School House by Spavinaw Creek. He said he really didn't know anything about the Bible, but the people didn't either, and his love and compassion must have shown through to them as there were 33 conversions. In 1936, Jake left his son, Howard, to help care for the farm and his wife, Callie and children, and walked to Arkansas for a series of revivals. At Kingston there were 105 conversions, and baptized 65 of them. A pool hall, whiskey store, and a beer joint closed. Five hundred persons attended the baptizing that followed the meeting. He also held revivals in the court houses of Berryville, and Eureka Springs. After eight weeks of revival, he had walked 300 miles and was carrying his offerings of $18.00, tied in a hankerchief. He built and pastored the Cole Free Will Baptist Church for eight years. Other pastorates were Lowery, for eight years, where he built a church; First FWB Church in Pryor for six years, resigning to go into full time evangelistic work. He preached revivals in 125 different churches in Oklahoma, Arkansas, Missouri, California, New Mexico, and Idaho.

Richard Henry Gallant
Birth:
May 22, 1945
Death:
Jan. 30, 1994
Arizona
Burial:
Oakland Cemetery,
Poteau,
Le Flore County, Oklahoma,
Plot: Section L

He was born in Boston, Massachusetts, but came to the state of Oklahoma. He pastored for a time the Poteau Free Will Baptist Church then became a staff member for the Hillsdale Free Will Baptist College in Moore, Oklahoma. He ran for the Senate in the state of Oklahoma but did not achieve his goal. He moved to the state of Arizona and developed Valley fever while there and died.

Shelby Van Greeson
Birth:
Dec. 30, 1933
Oklahoma,
Death:
Jun. 8, 2008
Oklahoma City,
Oklahoma County, Oklahoma
Burial:
Sunny Lane Cemetery,
Del City,
Oklahoma County, Oklahoma

He attended Oklahoma City schools, and Hillsdale College, and completed his Master's in Theology. He was also retired from the US Post Office. His last pastorate was First FWB Church in Oklahoma City.

Alva Preston Gumm
Birth:
Nov. 25, 1923
Oklahoma
Death:
Feb. 13, 2008
Oklahoma
Burial:
McMillan Cemetery
McMillan
Marshall County, Oklahoma

Honored as a minister and servant to his fellowman. His name was in a list of ministers in the Freewill

Bapt. State Association Minutes, 1982, as pastor of Murray Hill.He graduated Durant HS, and attended Southeastern State Teacher College in Durant before departing to work on the railroad.

He was inducted into the U.S. Army and served in Algeria and India before being discharged as a Master Sergeant in 1946.

Upon returning home, Alva married Lucille Cox on Nov. 14, 1947, in Ashdown, AR. He continued to attend college and graduated from Southeastern State College in 1959.

Mr. Gumm would later become the full-time preacher at Murray Hill Free Will Baptist Church, east of Colbert. He also served as Chaplain of the Oklahoma State Senate for a week in March 2007, as part of a celebration of his four decades in serving the ministry. Senators unanimously passed a resolution in his honor of his service to the Lord and his congregation. From his military service, to four decades in the pulpit, he helped a countless number of people.

He also worked for the Katy Railroad for nearly 50 years. He held various positions on the RR and at the hospital.

Johnie Eli Hale
Birth:
Nov. 4, 1924
Theodosia,
Ozark County,
Missouri

Death:
Jun. 23, 2008
Burial:
Wann Cemetery,Oologah,
Rogers County,
Oklahoma

He pastored three churches in Oklahoma, five in Arkansas and two in California. He organized the church in Mountain Home, Arkansas and also served under the State Mission Boards in Arkansas and California starting the churches in Ash Flat, Arkansas. and Anderson, California. He preached revivals in Oklahoma, Missouri, Arkansas, Michigan, and to supplement his income while he worked as a tile setter and had his own business in Mountain Home, Ark.

John R. "J.R." Hall
Birth:
Dec. 8, 1927
Pottawatomie County,

Oklahoma,
Death:
Oct. 18, 2004
Blanchard,
McClain County, Oklahoma
Burial:
Lexington Cemetery,
Lexington, Cleveland County,
Oklahoma, Plot: SW

He was an ordained minister of the Free Will Baptist Church. He had preached over fifty years, and always was successful. He served in the U.S. Navy with honor. They lived in California and Oklahoma where he pastored churches and he died while pastor at First Free Will Baptist Church, Blanchard, Oklahoma, where he had completed twenty years.

Lonnie Hall
Birth:
Oct. 18, 1912
Hercules,
Taney County, Missouri
Death:

Dec. 2, 2003 Sapulpa, Creek County,
Oklahoma,
Burial:
Green Hill Memorial Gardens Cemetery, Sapulpa, Creek County, Oklahoma

He preached at churches in Oklahoma and Texas.

Rev Clyde Arthur Hamar
Birth:
Sep. 5, 1906
Putnam
Dewey County
Oklahoma
Death:
Sep. 12, 1992
Enid
Garfield County
Oklahoma
Burial:
Mound Valley Cemetery
Thomas
Custer County
Oklahoma
Plot: 184-3-4

Ordained minister/pastor of Free Will Baptist churches. Pastored at Weatherford, OK when it was a mission; did other useful work.

Ralph Clayton Hampton, Sr
Birth:
Mar. 3, 1915
Oklahoma
Death:
Dec. 29, 1986 Pottawatomie
County, Oklahoma
Burial:
Resthaven
Memorial Park, Shawnee,
Pottawatomie County, Oklahoma

He was an Minister for Free Will Baptist all his life. Three of his sons all became ministers and professors. Ralph Clayton Jr, Charles Edgar, James A, Larry Don. FWB Ministers. Ralph, Jr, and Charles Edgar, became college professors. Larry was editor at Thomas Nelson, Randall House Publications, and ACE publications.

George Washington Hanks, Jr
Birth:
Nov. 23, 1872
Texas
Death:
Mar. 16, 1958
Keller, Carter Co., Oklahoma
Burial:
Keller Cemetery,
Carter County, Oklahoma

Inscription: Married Aug. 2, 1911

Ernest Harrison
Birth:
May 4, 1920
Henrietta, Oklahoma
Death:
Sep. 10, 1985
Henrietta, Oklahoma
Burial:
Henryetta Cemetery, Henryetta,
Okmulgee County, Oklahoma

He pastored churches in Oklahoma at Weleeka, Henrietta, McAlester, Allen, and other places. He held positions in his local District Associations wherever he lived, and was elected to the Clerk position of the State Sunday School Board. He was elected as Ass't moderator of the State Association in 1970. He was always actively engaged in the work of the ministry and church. While at Weleeka, he was burned badly in an accidental fire on his job, and it was doubtful for a while he would survive. He recovered and went right back to his ministry, serving faithfully until his death. He had a brother, Harold, who became a noted minister, and he also left a son, Ernest, Jr., who is a successful pastor and administrator.

Rev Arty Hearod
Birth:
Jun. 18, 1940
Gerty
Hughes County
Oklahoma
Death:
Jan. 23, 2016
Holdenville

Hughes County
Oklahoma
Burial:
Hearod Family Cemetery
Holdenville
Hughes County
Oklahoma
Plot: On their home place

The Rev. Arty Hearod, 75, of Holdenville, was the son of Joe Arty Hearod & Stella (Miller) Hearod. He was brought up and attended schools in Gerty, and was a 1958 graduate of Gerty High School. He moved with his family to California, where they lived a few years and worked on various farms. He returned to Holdenville and worked several years on the Ramsey Ranch, moved to Choctaw for a few years and in 1969 moved back to Holdenville, his home for the past 46 years. He married Marguerite Hicks on Dec. 17, 1971, in Sand Springs. They lived in Holdenville, where he drove a school bus and worked for the R.H.

Ramsey Lumber Company from 1971 until the store closed in the 1980s. One week following their wedding, he became pastor of Lone Grove Free Will Baptist Church in Scipio, their shared calling until his wife preceded him in death on Jan. 13, 2016. He was a leader in establishing the Kiamichi Free Will Baptist Association. He loved visiting with church family. His favorite things were farming and gardening, and he loved cows. His greatest love was his grandchildren. He was preceded in death by his wife, Marguerite; his parents, Joe and Stella Hearod; one son, Paul Hearod; granddaughter Koby Fiero; grandson, Cliff Rogers; parents-in-law, Oscar and Opal Hicks, and nephew, Wayne Hearod. Funeral services were at Lone Grove Free Will Baptist Church in Scipio with the Rev. Jim Lawrence officiating.

Elder William H. Hearron

Birth:
1882
Death:
1957
Burial:
Dibble Cemetery,
Dibble County,
Oklahoma

An early FWB minister. Great leader.

J. Arthur Hearron
Birth:
1905
Death:
1968
Burial:
Dibble Cemetery,
Dibble,
McClain County,
Oklahoma

A good preacher and singer. He was the son of Eld and Mrs. W.H. Hearron.

Robert Dean Hidde
Birth:
Oct. 23, 1950
Fort Smith
Sebastian County, Arkansas
Death:
Mar. 15, 2013
Tulsa
Tulsa County, Oklahoma
Burial:
Memorial Park Cemetery
Tulsa
Tulsa County, Oklahoma

Bob Hidde was born to Robert and Nadine Hidde in Ft. Smith, Arkansas. He graduated from Tulsa Central High School in 1968 and went on to obtain his Doctorate in Sacred Theology at Princeton University in Princeton, New Jersey. On July 3, 1969, he married Vicki Reynolds. They welcomed a daughter Leah, on August 6, 1971.Bob answered God's call to ministry and began preaching at the age of 15. He served as a Free Will Baptist pastor for over 40 years. Churches he served included First Free Will Baptist in Tulsa, West Tulsa Free Will Baptist in Tulsa, Madison Avenue Free Will Baptist in Tulsa, Rose Hill Free Will Baptist in Monticello, Ark, Ballews

Chapel Free Will Baptist in Grubbs, Ark, and most currently, Northside Free Will Baptist in Broken Arrow. He believed in being prepared for ministry at a moment's notice. Pastor Hidde was in ministry as the on-call chaplain for Ninde Funeral Home for 25 years, ministering to thousands of Tulsa families and beyond. Since 1999, he was the Managing Trustee for Memorial Park Cemetery. He served as the Moderator for the Tulsa Free Will Baptist Association and sat on the Credential Boards. He was the past President for the Oklahoma Personnel Consultants. He was also a member of the Tulsa Men's Club, the Tulsa Summit Club and the University of Arkansas Alumni Association. Along with his wife, Vicki, he owned and worked in their career development business, Resume Source, Inc., helping thousands of people and companies around the United States.

Rev Robert Luther Hidde
Birth:
Jun. 22, 1910
Death:
Jan. 25, 1999
Burial:
Memorial Park Cemetery
Tulsa
Tulsa County, Oklahoma

Ordained Free Will Baptist minister/pastor. Listed in State Association of 1982 roll of ministers.

Herbert Curtis Hogue
Birth:
Apr. 16, 1931
Roff
Pontotoc County, Oklahoma
Death:
Mar. 17, 2013
Oakman
Pontotoc County, Oklahoma
Burial:
Francis Cedar Grove Cemetery
Francis
Pontotoc County, Oklahoma

Curtis Hogue, 81, of Ada, at his home. He attended Steedman and Byng grade school and graduated from Byng High School. He attended Hillsdale Bible College in Moore. Mr. Hogue pastored Free Will Baptist Churches for many years. He operated a Christian Bookstore for 10 years and formerly owned and operated Yard Ornaments, Etc. Mr. Hogue was a longtime active member of the First Free Will Baptist Church in Ada where he taught Sunday School Class for over 50 years.

Henry S Huckeby
Birth:
May 8, 1858
Arkansas
Death:
Jan. 26, 1913
Garvin County, Oklahoma
Burial:
McGee Cemetery,
Stratford,
Garvin County
, Oklahoma,
Plot: Sect 3, Row 13

He was the son of George and Lucinda Huckeby, and was in Chickasaw Nation in the 1900 census with wife, Annice who he married 27 Apr. 1879 in Madison Co. AR. In the 1900-1901 Center Ass'n Minutes it is recorded "Rev. H.S. Huckeby as pastor at Summers Chapel" Maxwell, (Pontotoc Co) OK.

He was in a list of preacher's names the association accepted as ordained ministers after examination, and issued them a Certificate of Ordination showing they had recently come into the area.

In the 1902 session, he was elected to preach and then was elected to be Moderator. In 1908, he is credited with organizing the Non, FWB church, Hughes Co. OK, that produced so many FWB preachers just after statehood.

James D. Huling

Birth:
May 17, 1827
South New Berlin
Chenango County, New York
Death:
Nov. 6, 1900
Kingfisher County, Oklahoma
Burial:
Oak Grove Cemetery
Dove, Kingfisher County,
Oklahoma

Rev. J. D. Huling, whose parents were Daniel and Lydia (Burlingame) Huling, was born in Willett, Broome Co., N.Y., May 17, 1827. In September 1852, he was married to Mary W. Moore.

In 1870 he was ordained, and labored from 1870 to 1875 in connection with Rev. J. B. Fast in evangelistic work in the Cherokee Co. Quarterly Meeting.. In 1877 he organized the Caney church and with Brother Fast they organized the Montgomery Q.M., and also the church in Nevada, Kansas. Increasing infirmities prevented his holding a pastorate, but he still preached as opportunity offered and strength permitted.

Inscription:
"J. D. HULING,
CO.I., 15 ILL. INF."

Retes Hunsucker
Birth:
Feb. 22, 1928
Hoyt, Oklahoma
Death:
Sep. 23, 2002
Stillwater
Payne County,Oklahoma
Burial:
Fairlawn Cemetery
Stillwater
Payne County,Oklahoma
Plot: Blk-P2, Lot 6

He was born to Hiramm and Sammie Sallie (Busbee) Hunsucker. He married Lola Joyce Jones Dec. 30, 1947. After she died, he married Elsie Elvina (Bearry) Turner Sept. 2, 1989, in Eureka Springs, Ark.

He attended schools in the country area and worked on his parents' farm. He was one of 12 children. After completing six years of school, he was self-educated. He served two years in the Marine Corps. during the Korean War.

An ordained Free Will Baptist minister. His name in 1962 Minutes showed him with Silver City Church, near Tulsa. He preached for more than 30 years and pastored in four Freewill Baptist Churches. He was also a sewing machine salesman and sold storm shelters. He was a member of Highland Park Freewill Baptist Church.

Inscription:
Buried: 09/29/2002

Marion Leander "M.L." Hunt
Birth:
Feb. 26, 1859
Indiana
Death:
Apr. 23, 1938
Pontotoc County,
Oakman Cemetery
Oakman
Pontotoc County,Oklahoma

Son of John C. Hunt and Samantha S. (Round) HUNT. He married Ruth Harriet (Crump) Dec. 24, 1883, in Scott Co. AR. The moved to Indian Territory after 1890. Although not a minister, he was a deacon and a long-time member of the Free Will Baptist Center Association (Pontotoc Co. OK), and served as its first permanant clerk for many years.

His careful recordings were the basis for a concise history of its proceedings that was published in 1981, with Rev. Jimmy R. Nichols, Chairman of the committee, which history is dedicated to "M.L. Hunt, because of his dedication and service to this association." He also was one of the first Pontotoc County Commissioners.

Phillip "Phil" Iker
Birth:
Aug. 12, 1949
Allen
Pontotoc County,Oklahoma,
Death:
Jun. 29, 2012
Calvin
Hughes County,Oklahoma
Burial:
Calvin Cemetery
Calvin
Hughes County,Oklahoma

Listed in roll of OK Free Will Baptist state ministers in the 1982 State Association Minutes. He was pastor at Stuart at that time.

He served in Vietnam and also as mayor of Calvin. He was retired from the Army.

George M. Isham
Birth:
Sep. 9, 1848
Tennessee
Death:
Nov. 10, 1938
Henryetta,
Okmulgee County, Oklahoma
Burial:

Oakman Cemetery, Oakman, Pontotoc County, Oklahoma

He became a minister and joined the Free Will Baptist where he was found in Chickasaw Nation (Pontotoc Co. OK) by 1900. During the next several years he was active in the old Center Association, and his name appears in the Minutes of its meetings. He was elected its moderator in the 1900 session at Oakman Church. In this 1900 account, he was listed as pastor of Egypt Church, and Union Arbor at Midland, west of Ada. In 1902, he was pastor of four churches...one each Sunday. (This was frequently done then to supply the churches part of the time with a minister).These four churches were: Egypt, Summers Chapel, Union, and Union Arbor. His address was Ada, Indian Territory. In 1903, he was pastor of Oakman church. He was frequently called upon to preach at these meetings. He moved to Stephens Co, and 1920 census, he was a widower at age 67; by 1930.

Clarence Albert Jarrett
Birth:

Sep. 13, 1925
Missouri
Death:
Sep. 14, 2008
McAlester,
Pittsburg County, Oklahoma
Burial:
Tannehill Cemetery, McAlester,
Pittsburg County, Oklahoma

He joined the U.S. Navy and served during WWII in the Aleutian Island Campaign. Albert worked as an auto mechanic and painting contractor. He built and pastored Crowder Free Will Baptist Church, North McAlester Free Will Baptist Church and Fellowship Free Will Baptist Church in McAlester. He assisted with building other churches and was an active member of the Gaines Creek Free Will Baptist Association. He was a member of the American Legion and served as chaplain for the Harrison Powers Post #79 of McAlester for many years. He was a member of Canadian Shores Free Will Baptist Church.

Earl Jenson
Birth:
Jun. 18, 1911
Pittsburg County, Oklahoma
Death: Feb. 21, 1985
McAlester,
Pittsburg County, Oklahoma
Burial:
Indianola Cemetery,
Indianola, Pittsburg County,
Oklahoma
He was serving as pastor of the Lone Oak Free Will Baptist Church

at the time of his death. He was ordained as a Free Will Baptist Minister Aug. 14, 1943 and pastored churches in Oklahoma, California and Missouri.

Wade T. Jernigan
Birth:
Sep. 25, 1927
Bladenboro,
Bladen County, North Carolina
Death:
May 15, 2006
Tulsa, Tulsa County, Oklahoma,
Burial:
Willow View Cemetery,
Cleveland County, Oklahoma

The ministry of the well-known Free Will Baptist preacher and educator spanned more than 60 years. His education included an English Bible diploma, a bachelor of science of arts, a master's degree and doctorate in Theology. Five colleges and universities have conferred honorary degrees upon him. He was 17 when he announced his call to preach on March 25, 1945, at his home church, Oak Grove Church in Bladenboro, N. C. He was licensed to preach the following Sunday and preached his first sermon April 8, 1945, at Oak Grove Church. He has conducted more than 800 revivals, pastored 14 churches including the First Free Will Baptist Church in Miami, and served four churches as interim pastor. He was involved in church pioneering and was instrumental in starting 25 churches. He was referred to across the United States as "Mr. Free Will Baptist." He helped start Oklahoma Bible College (now Hillsdale Free Will Baptist College), and was a member of the Christian Education Board. Most recently, he served as a Professor of Homiletics and in Public Relations with the office of Institutional Advancement at Hillsdale Free Will Baptist College. Jernigan's bold style and gift for doctrinal preaching made him a popular conference and revival speaker. He was a leader wherever he served: Moderator of the Oklahoma State Association, Executive Secretary of the California State Association, Chairman of the national Home Missions Board, member of the Commission on Theological Liberalism, Home Missionary to Idaho, member of both the national General Board and Executive Committee. Wade was a member of the five-man committee that recommended starting in 1958 what is now Hillsdale FWB College. However, his signature work in education came during a nine-year span (1969-1978) when he served as president of California Christian College in Fresno. A prolific writer, Jernigan produced four books, including his best-known work published in 1975, *The Unsealed Book, an Amillennial commentary on the Book of Revelation.* He also wrote 60 songs, poetry, and numerous articles.

Scott Jones
Birth:
Aug. 8, 1910
Death:
Jan. 15, 1976
Burial:
Francis Cedar Grove Cemetery,
Francis,
Pontotoc County, Oklahoma

William Chapman "Bud" Jones
Birth:
Feb. 3, 1856
Death:
Sep. 5, 1944
Burial:
Rosedale Cemetery,
Ada, Pontotoc County, Oklahoma,
Plot: West-26-5-5

A minister and son-in-law of Rev. Ransom Bess.

George Earl Judd
Birth:
Mar. 9, 1915
Death:
Feb. 21, 1989
Burial:
Sub-Station Cemetery,
Freedom, HillCreek County,
Oklahoma

He served as a PVT.in the U.S. Army during World War Two.

Oh, may I join the choir invisible Of those immortal dead who live again.

Myrl Floyd Kellett
Birth:
Jan. 18, 1926
Antlers
Pushmataha County
Oklahoma, USA
Death:
Jan. 25, 2015
Lawton
Comanche County
Oklahoma
Burial:
Sunset Memorial Gardens
Lawton
Comanche County
Oklahoma

He became a Christian in February 1956 at Trinity Baptist Church, Lawton. He and Wanda became members of the First Free Will Baptist Church on April 20, 1958. He served as Sunday School Superintendent and in various other capacities. In July 1960 he and a small band of Christians organized and established the Brockland Free Will Baptist Church, Lawton. On September 8, 1962 he was licensed to preach the Gospel in the Dibble Association of Free Will Baptist, then on September 7, 1963 he was ordained as a Free Will Baptist Minister. In May 1965 he became the Pastor of the First Free Will Baptist Church and was pastor until 1970. During this Pastoral work there was a new sanctuary built. He evangelized all over Kansas, Arkansas, Texas and Oklahoma. He was also the Associate Pastor at Brockland Free Will Baptist Church from April 1975 through August 1977. Again in February 1979 he became the Pastor of the First Free Will Baptist Church and was there for 34 years. He was blessed to see his vision with the completion of the educational facility built. Over the years there have been many saved, many baptized and those who surrendered to preach the Gospel. He counted it a privilege to be a servant of the Lord Jesus Christ. He was involved in all phases of the Free Will Baptist work. He served in different capacities in the Hopewell No. 2 Association of Free Will Baptist and in the Dibble Association of Free Will Baptist. He supported the work of the Free Will Baptist in the State of Oklahoma and the National Free Will Baptist as well.

Live For Eternity
God Esteems And
Calls

Richard P. Kennedy
Birth:
Oct. 10, 1949
Richmond,
Contra Costa County, California
Death:
Aug. 10, 2012
Owasso,
Tulsa County, Oklahoma
Burial:
Graceland Memorial
Park Cemetery, Owasso,
Tulsa County, Oklahoma

Dr. Kennedy served in the ministry of Jesus Christ for 30 years. His formal education began at California Christian College in Fresno, California, where he received his Bachelor of Science Degree. He continued his education at Golden Gate Baptist Seminary in Mill Valley, California, where he began his Master of Divinity Studies.
He then attended Liberty University in Lynchburg, Virginia, and completed his Masters and his Doctor of Ministry at Fuller Theological Seminary in Pasadena, California. Always venturesome,

Dr. Kennedy began two churches; Temple Church, Greenville, North Carolina, and Northside Church, Stockton, California. Both grew at record rates and continue to impact people's lives around the world. He was Co-Pastor at Big Valley Grace Community Church in Modesto, California, for seven years and ended his career as head pastor of Los Gatos Christian Church, Los Gatos, California. Dr. Kennedy also served as an adjunct professor for Oklahoma Wesleyan University and Hillsdale Free Will Baptist College.

Bob L. Ketchum
Birth:
Jul. 30, 1936
Liberty,
Tulsa County, Oklahoma
Death:
Feb. 28, 2010
Tulsa,
Tulsa County, Oklahoma
Burial:
Bixby Cemetery, Bixby,
Tulsa County, Oklahoma

Bob received and accepted the call to the ministry during his teenage years, preaching his first sermon in May 1953 at Shahan. Shortly after ordination in 1955, he was asked to preach two Sundays each month at Duck Creek Church and twice monthly at Hitchita Free Will Baptist Church. His pastorates included Okmulgee, Cushing, and Shady Grove in Tennessee, Central in Tulsa, Owasso and Grace North of Indian Springs, Broken Arrow. He served the Lord as founder, then pastor of Grace for 25 years. During his years of pastoring, he served the Free Will Baptist denomination in various positions. For several years he was a member of the Board of Trustees of Free Will Baptist College in Nashville, TN, his alma mater. He was selected to preach at the Free Will Baptist National Convention at Macon, Georgia in 1973. He also was privileged to serve the Oklahoma Free Will Baptists on several boards and committees during these years and two as the state moderator.

William O. "Bill" Ketchum
Birth:
Unknown
Death:
Jul. 15, 2004
Oklahoma
Burial:
Prairie Gardens Cemetery,
Liberty,
Tulsa County, Oklahoma

The Rev. Bill Ketchum, 86, of Bixby, an ordained Free Will Baptist minister for many years. He pastored churches and was used extensively as an evangelist. (Sapulpa Herald)

John Dudley Kimbrough
Birth:
Nov. 17, 1880
Alabama
Death:
Jan. 3, 1958
Oklahoma
Burial:
Allen Cemetery,
Allen, Pontotoc County,
Oklahoma

John D. Kimbrough was an ordained Free Will Baptist minister, where and when he was ordained is unknown, but probably as a very young man. He was one of those who preached and ministered in Indian Territorial days (before 1907) and afterward. No record is available that tells the number that he baptized, churches organized, weddings or funerals that he was the officiant, but he is acknowledged by descendants of those who knew him that he was well-loved, engaged in his work and did a great service for his Master. His name and picture in the book, *"History of the First Hundred Years 1908-2008,"* show his name is still honored today for his labors. In the *"Annuals of Red Oak*, pg 153, his name is listed with a few other ministers that preached at the Norris FWB church, even back to 1890's.

Richard G. Lane
Birth:
Feb. 28, 1896
Texas
Death:
Jun. 16, 1959
Arkansas
Burial:
Little Cemetery, Little,
Seminole County, Oklahoma

He was a Free Will Baptist minister and pastor from Sulphur, Oklahoma. Much of his ministry was in central Arkansas at the Pleasant Grove Free Will Baptist Church in Greenbrier and later he organized the First Free Will Baptist Church in Conway. His daughter, Jean, was the wife of J. Reford Wilson who became the National Director for Foreign Missions in Nashville Tennessee for the National Association of Free Will Baptists.

He was the authors pastor when he was a boy. Mom Lane impacted me dearly. Their son-in-law, J.Reford Wilson conducted our marriage. A godly couple to whom I owe my early Bible instruction. They were a great indian couple from Oklahoms who ministered in my church many years in Arkansas. "Mom" Lane taught me in SS to tithe 4 years before I was saved. She taught to trust in God fully.

Harry L. Lee
Birth:
Feb. 11, 1914

Death:
Nov. 19, 1996
Burial:
Arpelar Cemetery
Arpelar, Pittsburg County,
Oklahoma

Ordained Free Will Baptist minister/pastor. He pastored churches in his locality, while also being bi-vocational, and helping others. He was a quiet, mild-mannered man, who was esteemed by all who knew him.

"What shall be the end of all covetous persons?
—Eternal damnation."

John Alvin Lee
Birth:
Sep., 1862
Illinois
Death:
Jun. 4, 1951
Pontotoc County, Oklahoma
Burial:
Francis Cedar Grove Cemetery,
Francis,
Pontotoc County, Oklahoma

John moved to Oklahoma in 1887. Elder Lee was ordained a Free Will Baptist minister in 1894. His name appears often in old church records, having served as pastor of several churches, and moderator of the Center Association in 1900. He preached, performed weddings, conducted funerals, and was active in revival work.

William E Lindsey
Birth:
1873
Death:
Jul. 24, 1945
Burial:
Oak Park Cemetery, Chandler,
Lincoln County, Oklahoma,
Plot: Section 9, Lot 69

He was a FWB pastor in the early years.

John W. Lunsford
Birth:
Apr. 21, 1850
Tennessee
Death:
May 17, 1928
Oklahoma
Burial:
West Hill Cemetery,
Roff, Pontotoc County, Oklahoma
John was a Free Will Baptist minister in the old Center Ass'n, (Pontotoc Co)of churches where he is shown to have pastored various churches. In 1912, he was pastor at Shady Grove, Dolberg, Pontotoc Co. He had a brother, W.G. Lunsford, also a minister

listed in the names of a committee in a 1902 meeting, of this same Center Association.

Marvin Kenneth Mann
Birth:
Sep. 19, 1928
Briartown
Muskogee County, Oklahoma
Death:
Jul. 14, 2013
Tulsa
Tulsa County, Oklahoma
Burial:
Greenlawn Cemetery
Checotah
McIntosh County, Oklahoma

His life was service to his Lord and Savior Jesus Christ, to love on his family and serve with his church family. He enjoyed golf and raising cattle. He was preceded in death by his parents, Rev. LW and Lula Belle Mann. He honorably served our nation in the United States Army and was proud to be a veteran. Along with his brother Bill, he started Ace Fence Company in November 1953 in which he operated until his retirement in 1990. He and a brother planted churches and denominational associations and in the early days preached revivals together. They labored together. He was ordained as a preacher of the gospel on September 11, 1960 in Broken Arrow, OK. The fruit from the churches planted and many souls led to Christ will only be fully known in Heaven. After years of pastorates, he cherished being the moderator of the Arkansas Valley Association of Free Will Baptist as well as serving in the General Board of the Oklahoma Association of Free Will Baptist. He preached his last sermon one week before his home-going. He was thrilled to see his grandsons continue his passion of church-planting in Texas and Illinois.

David T. Mansker
Birth:
Jun. 4, 1847
Johnson County, Arkansas
Death:
Mar. 6, 1929
Paden, Okfuskee County,
Oklahoma
Burial:
Lambdin, Prague,
Lincoln County, Oklahoma

His great-grandfather was George Mansker, born about 1747 in Germany; his grandfather was William Mansker, born about 1774 in Pennsylvania; and his father was John R. Mansker, born in Tennessee. During the 1830s, the Manskers moved from Tennessee to Arkansas. By 1834, Thomas Mansker's father and mother were married in Lawrence County, Arkansas, one of the first counties to be settled in the state. By at least 1836, they had moved into Johnson County, Arkansas, where Tom was born on the 4th of June 1847. When he was 17, and at the point of enlistment, all the males of his family were already active in military service except for his youngest brother. Tom Mansker enlisted into the 7th Missouri Cavalry of the Confederate States of America. Tom was assigned to Captain Nathan Horn's Company, Lieutenant Colonel C. H. Nichol's Regiment of Colonel Sidney D. Jackman's Brigade under General Sterling Price. The Manskers came into Indian Territory probably after

September 1891 to an area opened up to White settlement. Sometime between 1900 and 1910, David Thomas Mansker received his call and appointment to the ministry, a calling he pursued to the end of his life. Sometime between 1910 and 1920, Tom Mansker and his wife Martha Jane moved to Ontario, Malheur County, Oregon. However, before another two years had passed, they were back in Oklahoma, but this time in Paden, Okfuskee County, Oklahoma. In the obituary of Martha it read, "They lived and bore the trials and hardships of the early life of Oklahoma. She was converted about the age of 27 and ever afterwards lived a beautiful devoted Christian life, her companion being a minister of the gospel of the Free Will Baptist Church. "Reverend McElvaney officiated. Published in The Prague Record, Thursday, November 17, 1921. Seven and a half years after her death, the Rev. Mansker died in Paden, and was buried beside Martha Jane. After the funeral, Elder Epperson wrote these words about his friend and colleague: David Thomas Mansker "came nearer being loved by everybody than any man I ever knew. He had been preaching some forty years, after having come to Oklahoma in an early day. He was as faithful to his church as he was to his family. You can't say too much for him as a man or as a minister—he was the best pastor I think I ever saw. To make it plain, it will take all eternity to tell about Brother Mansker. We know where to find him. Oh, I could say so much, but he will tell us all about it over there." ("Obituary for Elder David Thomas Mansker", published in The Free Will Baptist Gem, April 1929, p. 12)On his next birthday, he would have been 82 years old. The funeral was held in the Free Will Baptist Church in Paden. Several preachers were in attendance and had a part in the funeral. The services were conducted by Elder A. B. Epperson. Reverend McElvany, of Prague, a life-long friend of Tom's, talked at the gravesite.

Inscription:
Co. C. Mo. Cav. CSA

Leona Mae Churchill Mayfield
Birth:
May 15, 1882
Kansas
Death:
May 20, 1948
Lincoln County, Oklahoma
Burial:
Iowa Chapel Cemetery
Lincoln County, Oklahoma

Parents:Menzo Churchill (1843 - 1922)-Sarah Violetta Clarke Churchill (1853 - 1933). Spouse: Rufus Mayfield (1879 - 1960).Children: Orial C. Mayfield (1905 - 1975), Rex V Mayfield (1911 - 1993), Otis Clyde Mayfield (1919 - 1987).

Early Oklahoma lady preacher.

Lester James Maynard
Birth:
Mar. 3, 1915
Death:
Jun. 27, 2002
Burial:
Blanchard Cemetery,
Blanchard,
McClain County,
Oklahoma

He was a minister over 50 years.

Alvis Lee McAffrey
Birth:
Sep. 23, 1914
McGee, Garvin County,
Oklahoma
Death:
Nov. 9, 1994
Madill, Marshall County,
Oklahoma
Burial:
Woodberry Forest Cemetery,
Madill, Marshall County,
Oklahoma

He was ordained a Free Will Baptist minister when a young man, and then pastored churches throughout the area, among them were Stratford, Gaar Corner, and a long pastorate at First Free Will Baptist Church in Sulphur; Non FWB, and Memorial at Sulphur. He was a minister for over 50 years. He served on boards for his association and was active in the Oklahoma State Association of FWB.

Furman Archie McCage
Birth:
Nov. 22, 1907
Stigler, Haskell County, Oklahoma
Death:
Dec. 29, 1972
Oklahoma City, Oklahoma County,
Oklahoma
Burial:
Stigler Cemetery, Stigler,
Haskell County, Oklahoma

Ordained Free Will Baptist minister/pastor in Oklahoma and California where he held various positions in the denomination.

Rev Millard "Preach" McGuire
Birth:
Jul. 19, 1931
Kellyville
Creek County
Oklahoma
Death:
Mar. 19, 2015
Kellyville
Creek County
Oklahoma
Burial:
Sunrise Cemetery
Kellyville
Creek County
Oklahoma

Millard "Preach" McGuire, 83 years, 8 months, and 3 days, went to be with the Lord at his home in Kellyville.

Reverend McGuire was preceded in death by his parents, Clint and Willie McGuire; his brothers, Marvin "Winks" Eugene McGuire and Melvin Verlin McGuire; and his eldest son, Darrell Eugene McGuire.

Joshua E. "J.E." McGee
Birth:
Sep. 20, 1857
Fayette County, Alabama
Death:
Jan. 21, 1923
Oklahoma,
Burial:
Garwin Cemetery, Antlers,
Pushmataha County, Oklahoma

Eld. J.E. McGee was a pioneer Free Will Baptist minister in the Indian Territory and after statehood until his death. He was a great evangelist who did a great work in the Choctaw Nation. In 1885, he began a work at CullaChaha, near Cameron, and was one of the founders of the Old Territorial Association organized at Nubbin Ridge, near Spiro, Oklahoma, in 1894. The boundaries were from 18 miles west of Tahlequah, to the Arkansas line at Fort Smith and south to Antlers. Later, the growth produced two associations, and one carried the name, Roberts-McGee, after two of the founding fathers.

Dottis McGehee

Birth:
Jan. 29, 1881 Thackerville, Love County,
Oklahoma
Death:
Sep. 26, 1939
Pontotoc County,
Oklahoma
Burial:
Oakman Cemetery,
Oakman,
Pontotoc County,
Oklahoma

Rev. McGehee was ordained a Free Will Baptist minister in 1927 (per old minutes) of the Center Association where he chiefly labored.

Cecil E. McKenzie

Birth:
Aug. 14, 1902
Death:
Apr. 19, 1976
Burial:
Holdenville Cemetery,
Holdenville, Hughes County,
Oklahoma

Martin M McKee

Birth:
Oct. 1, 1889
Nelson, Choctaw County
Oklahoma
Death:
Nov. 14, 1947
Paris, Lamar County, Texas
Burial:
Soper Cemetery, Soper,
Choctaw County, Oklahoma

He was an ordained Free Will Baptist minister, who preached, pastored, baptized and performed weddings all over southeastern Okla. in the 1920-1940's. He was active in Associational meetings, often writing an article about it for a church publication. His name appears in old records of the church. In 1929, he was elected Moderator of the Oklahoma State Ass'n of FWB. We know he was a beloved and faithful minister. He died in a Paris, TX hospital.

Death Is Not The Greatest Loss In Life.

The Greatest Loss Is What Dies Inside Us While We Live.

Rev John Metcalf
Birth:
Jun. 4, 1957
Death:
Feb. 28, 1984
Burial:
Ridgelawn Cemetery
Collinsville
Tulsa County
Oklahoma

A Free Will Bapt. missionary-appointee to South America., when he and wife, M. Kaye, were killed in a tragic car accident in Tenn. A great loss. Spouse: Melinda Kay Dudley Metcalf (1958 - 1984)

Edward E Morris
Birth:
Jun. 8, 1897
Arkansas
Death:
Feb., 1987
Oklahoma City
Oklahoma County, Oklahoma
Burial:
Memorial Park Cemetery,
Ada, Pontotoc County, Oklahoma

E. E. Morris, was born in Arkansas, but soon was living in Oklahoma. He served in the U.S. Army in WWI. He was an ordained Free Will Baptist minister and pastored churches in Oklahoma and California for many years pastoring the Ada First FWB for several years in the 1930-40's, then the Capitol Hill FWB Church, in Oklahoma City, where it grew and he carried on a weekly radio program. He was used as an evangelist frequently. He served on State Boards and also in local Districts. He served a term as the moderator of the National Association in its early days. He was a promoter of the denominational enterprises. He pastored in California where his wife, died in 1957. He later served as California

State Promotional Director. He pastored other churches at Tulare and Arvin, California. He was known for his strong positions on issues he believed in and was a leader in those things. He was a "hands on" pastor, frequently using a carpenter's tools to get a job finished.

J C Morgan
Birth:
May 6, 1931
Death:
Aug. 23, 2013
Burial:
Bixby Cemetery
Bixby
Tulsa County, Oklahoma

Shortly after High school, J. C. married the love of his life, Lila Fay James in Bixby Oklahoma. In those early years J.C. worked as a welder for Yuba Heat Transfer and McNamara Tank in Tulsa.

J.C. was led to Christ by Reverend Ray Gwartney at the Bixby Free Will Baptist Church. He became an ordained minister in December of 1961. Shortly thereafter he accepted his first pastorate at Pensacola Free Will Baptist church near Grand Lake. Under his guidance and Lila Faye's support, the church grew and thrived. In the early 1960's the family moved to Oklahoma City where he and Lila Faye managed the Free Will Baptist Bible book store. J.C. attended the Hillsdale Free Will Baptist Bible College at night during this time, and honed his preaching style at numerous small churches throughout Oklahoma. The Lord led J.C. to Pastor Churches in Chickasha and Lawnwood Free Will Baptist church in Tulsa, where he retired. After his retirement in the mid 1990's, J.C. and Lila Faye returned to their hometown of Bixby where they continued to serve in local churches. All in all he preached over 4,000 sermons, and hundreds of baptisms, funerals and weddings. He always challenged young people to trust God and live the Christian life. In retirement, he served as an interim pastor at Lewis Avenue Free Will Baptist church. In the past few years he has served in various roles, including the senior's ministry at the Bixby Free Will Baptist church.

Rev W. E. Mullendore
Birth:
Sep. 5, 1912
Death:
Oct. 24, 1999
Burial:

Resthaven Memorial Park
Shawnee
Pottawatomie County
Oklahoma

An ordained FWB Minister and pastor.

B C Munkus
Birth:
Nov. 20, 1876
Ellis County, Texas
Death:
Sep. 15, 1952
Norman, Cleveland County, Oklahoma
Burial:
Moore Cemetery, Moore, Cleveland County, Oklahoma

He left home at an early age, and moved to the Oklahoma Indian Territory before 1900. He was a Free Will Baptist minister & evangelist and was active in the early years of the Oklahoma FWB State Association.

Rev Clifford C. Myers
Birth:
May 27, 1930
Williams
Le Flore County
Oklahoma
Death:
Mar. 12, 2014
Pocola
Le Flore County, Oklahoma
Burial:
Greenhill Cemetery
Cameron
Le Flore County, Oklahoma

He was the founding pastor of Pocola Heights Free Will Baptist Church in 1971 where he served as pastor until his death, having been a minister for 57 years, a retired truck driver, and a baseball coach. Born to Andrew Jackson and Nora Isabel (Byrd) Myers.

Rev Clifford Garlan Myers
Birth:
Jun. 22, 1904
Cabaniss
Pittsburg County
Oklahoma
Death:
Jan. 17, 1992
McAlester
Pittsburg County
Oklahoma
Burial:
Hugh Low Cemetery
Pittsburg County
Oklahoma

FREE WILL BAPTIST MINISTERS BURIED IN OKLAHOMA

Clifford Garlen Myers was the son of Miles Travis and Claudia Sarah Swilling Myers.

He was an ordained Free Will Baptist Minister and pastored churches in Pittsburg Co. and in eastern Oklahoma, Lone Grove and others. He attended state meetings and raised a nice family.

John Columbus Newby
Birth:
Oct. 30, 1884
Arkansas
Death:
Aug. 12, 1957
Le Flore County, Oklahoma
Burial:
Ellis Chapel Cemetery, Wister,
Le Flore County, Oklahoma

Newby, known affectionately as "Clum" Newby, was an ordained Free Will Baptist minister. When he came from Arkansas to Indian Territory he soon found and worked with others of like faith, such as Eld. J.M. Roberts, who in 1894, gathered some of them together to form a Territorial Association. An old Latimer Co. record, *"Annals of Red Oak"*, page 153, we find his name among the earliest ministers, alone with Wilson Yandell, Rouche Allen, Mr. West, Clum (Columbus) Newby, Jack Shipman and Elzie Yandell, who preached at Norris Church (outside Red Oak) as early as 1890. We find his name in old minutes, where he preached and organized churches all over eastern Oklahoma. He was in the group of ministers who helped form the State Association of FWB, in 1908, at Holdenville, (Hughes Co) Oklahoma.

Dennis H O'Donnell
Birth:
Oct. 17, 1907
Death:
Sep. 3, 1991
Burial:
Little Cemetery, Little,
Seminole County, Oklahoma

A Free Will Baptist minister and pastor.(Bro. to Rev. E. A. O'Donnell).

If You Spend All Your Time Worrying About Dying, Living Isn't Going To Be Much Fun.

Emris Allen O'Donnell
Birth:
Feb. 9, 1900
St. Clair County, Alabama
Death:
Mar., 1979
Holdenville,
Hughes County, Oklahoma
Burial:
Fairlawn Cemetery, Chickasha,
Grady County, Oklahoma,
Plot: Blk 5 Lt 14 Sp 8 SE/4

He was an ordained minister of the Free Will Baptists. He pastored FWB churches in Oklahoma where he was involved in their ministries, serving in various positions, and was editor of a state church paper, *"The Gospel Truth"* at one time. He had a great singing and speaking voice, and a pleasant personality. He was a WW I veteran.

James Montgomery Pannell
Birth:
Jun. 3, 1856
Tishomingo County, Mississippi
Death:
Jul. 16, 1909
Pontotoc County, Oklahoma
Burial:
Maxwell Cemetery, Oil Center,
Pontotoc County, Oklahoma

Parents were Bartlet Pannell Cecilla. Married to Nancy Melvina Burgess 6 April 1877. An ordained minister in the Free Will Baptist Center Association, Pontotoc/Garvin counties. His death is recorded in its old Minutes. Nancy Ann Melvina Burgess Pannell (1857 - 1941).

FREE WILL BAPTIST MINISTERS BURIED IN OKLAHOMA

Isaac Newton Pate
Birth:
Dec. 22, 1870
Pike County, Arkansas
Death:
Jun. 22, 1951
Antlers, Pushmataha County,
Oklahoma
Burial:
Antlers City Cemetery,
Antlers, Pushmataha County,
Oklahoma

Pate was a pioneer Free Will Baptist preacher in Oklahoma.

Rev George Pettyjohn
Birth:
Feb. 19, 1914
Death:
Dec. 15, 1992
Burial:
Resthaven Gardens Cemetery
Oklahoma City
Cleveland County
Oklahoma

Ordained Free Will Bapt. minister, serving churches in Okla. County and others. He also sang with feeling.
He served as a SSgt US Marine Corps in the S. Pacific, Guam, Guadalcanal islands, which time he was pinned down. They had to fight their way out. He lived to come home, then surrendered to preach the gospel, which he did for years.

David Leroy Poynor
Birth:
Jul. 3, 1820
Death:
Nov. 12, 1903
Burial:
Shahan Cemetery
Broken Arrow
Wagoner County, Oklahoma

A leader in the early beginnings in NW AR/MO for his church and association of churches. Raised a large family.

Johnny H. Priest
Birth:
Dec. 30, 1920 Non, Hughes County,
Oklahoma
Death:
Dec. 16, 1988
Boise City,

Cimarron County, Oklahoma
Burial:
McGee Cemetery,
Stratford,
Garvin County, Oklahoma

He entered WWII military service and served his country. He announced his call to preach in the Free Will Baptist Church of Non and began to preach in area churches. He began a Free Will Baptist Church in the panhandle of Oklahoma at Boise City.

Rev J. R. Proctor
Birth:
Aug. 26, 1924
Death:
Jul. 20, 2003
Burial:
Graceland Memorial Park
Rogers County, Oklahoma

Ordained Free Will Bapt. minister/pastor.

Rev Susie Loggains Pruitt
Birth:
Feb. 17, 1895
Arkansas
Death:
Sep. 3, 1987
Tulsa, Tulsa County, Oklahoma
Burial:
Park Grove Cemetery,

Broken Arrow
Tulsa County, Oklahoma, USA
Plot: Section I, Block 17, Lot 2,
Space 3

Susie was the daughter of Charlie Loggains and was born in Arkansas. She married John Robert Pruitt in Carroll County, Arkansas on Dec. 24, 1913 and was the first ordained female minister in the Freewill Baptist Church in that area.. She died at Tulsa, Oklahoma at the age of 92.

Rev Mark D. Purdom
Birth:
1859
Death:
1941
Burial:
McLain Cemetery
Muskogee
Muskogee County
Oklahoma

FWB minister and his son, Ulis C. Purdom (1906 - 1989) was also.

Inscription:
Asleep in Jesus

Father, into thy hands I commend my spirit."

Luke 23:46

Ulis C. Purdom
Birth:
Jan. 8, 1906
Piette, Arkansas
Death:
Aug. 16, 1989
Quinton, Pittsburg County,
Oklahoma
Burial: McLain Cemetery
Muskogee,
Muskogee County,
Oklahoma

He was an ordained FWB minister, and his name appears in old minutes, and in 1966, he was the District evangelist for Gaines Creek Association. His parents were M. D. Purdom (1859 - 1941) and Louisa Purdom (1865 - 1952) and his wife was Cora Brumley Purdom (1913 - 1978)

Raymond Odell Qualls
Birth:
Mar. 6, 1927
Mulberry, Crawford County,
Arkansas
Death:
Nov. 24, 2001
Fort Smith, Sebastian County,
Arkansas
Burial:
Maple Cemetery
Maple, Sequoyah County,
Oklahoma

Funeral services for Rev. Raymond QUALLS, 74, of Muldrow, were held Wednesday, at 10 a.m. at the Eastside Freewill Baptist Church, with Revs. Wade Jernigan, Gilbert Pixley and Jerry Copeland officiating. His wife was Lona Mae Viles Qualls (1929 - 2011).

James W "Jim" Ragland
Birth:
Oct. 10, 1864
Tennessee
Death:
Oct. 23, 1950
Oklahoma
Burial:
Oakman Cemetery,
Oakman, Pontotoc County
Oklahoma

A Free Will Baptist pioneer minister, ordained in 1919, serving in the Center Association of churches (Pontotoc Co. OK) as its moderator in 1899. He held various offices of leadership through 1934.

What a day that will be

When my savior I shall see!

Ellis F Reger
Birth:
Feb. 23, 1877
Death:
May 2, 1930
Burial:
Tecumseh Cemetery
Tecumseh
Pottawatomie County
Oklahoma, USA

His spouse was Olive Arizona Smith Reger (1880 - 1957) and they had six Children: Rev. Luster A Reger (1900 - 1950); Herman True Reger (1906 - 1994); Edna B. Reger Leach (1914 - 2007); Clifford F Reger (1919 - 1991); Derril Lee Reger (1921 - 1921) and Corlene Olive Reger (1922 - 1938).

William Clay Richey
Birth:
Jan. 29, 1904
Aspermont,
Stonewall County, Texas
Death:
Sep. 3, 1961
Blanchard,
McClain County, Oklahoma
Burial:
Dibble Cemetery, Dibble,
McClain County, Oklahoma

He moved with his family from Texas to Oklahoma, attended schools and grew to manhood in around Grady and McClain counties, Oklahoma. He yielded his life to God's call to the gospel ministry in 1933 at once began "to preach Christ" in the local churches. He was ordained in the Free Will Baptist Church in 1933. He studied the scriptures assiduously, while gaining knowledge of parliamentary law, greatly aiding his denomination in its conference deliberations, he being selected to be the 'parliamentarian' for several sessions. He ably served the Oklahoma. State Association of FWB as moderator for several years, and his name appears in their minutes in other positions where he served. He was a good speaker and preacher. He reasoned the scriptures and had a forceful delivery. He was esteemed among his peers. In 1959, he preached the funeral of his old mentor, Dr. I.W. Yandell, in Oklahoma City. He pastored churches at Dibble, Bryant, Springhill (at Lexington), and Pleasant Hill churches, and organized the First Church at Blanchard, before he died suddenly.

They rest from their labors

W. G. Ridge
Birth:
May 25, 1856
Death:
Apr. 3, 1937
Burial:
Laverty Cemetery, Chickasha,
Grady County, Oklahoma

Tombstone has his name as Rev. W.G. Ridge

Albert S. Roberts
Birth:
May 7, 1877
Death:
Mar. 22, 1937
Burial:
Palestine Cemetery
Russellville, Pittsburg County,
Oklahoma

He was the grandson of Olive Branch Roberts from North Carolina. Olive Branch had 16 children and one was named Pleasant, John Pleasant who was a N.C. state legislator for over 20 years. John Pleasant moved to Arkansas and had five children. His baby's name was Albert Slayton, born in 1879. He had six children and the youngest was Rev. William Thomas Roberts.

James M. Roberts
Birth:
Jul. 20, 1852
Death:
Dec. 26, 1940

Burial:
Garland Cemetery, Stigler,
Haskell County, Oklahoma

Elder Roberts was an early Oklahoma pioneer Free Will Baptist preacher from Arkansas. His own words from old letters and diaries best describe his life and labors. "In the year of 1884 I moved from Sebastian County, Arkansas to the Cherokee Nation near Weber Falls on the Arkansas River, rented a farm, and soon began preaching on Saturdays and Sundays in the little school houses here and there and underbrush arbors and shade trees. I had a wife and seven children at that time, for which I made a living on the farm, so it took a lot of my time. I had an appointment ten miles north of Weber's Falls near McClain at the old Buckhorn schoolhouse and other places too numerous to mention. In 1892 Brother O .J. Tailor (Taylor), a Free Will Baptist preacher from Texas, located near McClain and I soon formed his acquaintance, and we began preaching together. In the latter part of 1892, he and I organized the Concord Church at the old Buckhorn school house which was the first Free Will Baptist church organized in the Cherokee nation. Bro. Tailor and I worked together for six years and organized churches in many places." He wrote, "These were trying times. There was no money, no roads, and no bridges." Elder Roberts made many of these long trips on foot while carrying his Bible and a change of clothing in a small satchel. Many times he waded the streams, even in winter. Sometimes he slept with his Bible for a pillow and his bed a pile of leaves or grass with the pale moon and the twinkling stars as a covering."The second church to be organized was the old 'Fields Chapel' Church Northeast of Porum, Oklahoma. It was then Star Villa, I.T. In 1885, another church was organized at old Cullachaha near Cameron in the Choctaw Nation, and Elder J. E. McGee began a work in that part of the country." A group of churches gathered near the old Scullvill Stant, in 1894 in the Choctaw part at a little school house known as Nubbin Ridge. There they were organized as the Territorial Association. But it was not perfected until Sept. 1894. Roberts was in the very formation of the Oklahoma FWB.

William Thomas Roberts
Birth:
Dec. 17, 1910
Mena,
Polk County, Arkansas
Death:
Mar. 29, 2000
Tulsa County,
Oklahoma
Burial:
Floral Haven Memorial Gardens,
Broken Arrow,
Tulsa County,
Oklahoma

Rev. Tommy Roberts was born to Rev. Albert Slayton Roberts and Nora Roberts. His father took his family from Arkansas to Oklahoma after their baby son, William Thomas was born.

Tommy resisted the call of God on his life, but at the age of 19 he accepted the Lord as Savior and the calling to preach God's Word. He married Lucy Marie Laughlin when he was 19 and she was 15. They had six children. When he passed away on March 29, 2000 he was probably the oldest FWB minister in Oklahoma at that time with 70 years of ministry and marriage.

He and his wife, Marie, pastored churches in Oklahoma, Kansas and California.

He "pastored" four churches at a time in the Stigler area. Some of them met in school houses with pot-bellied stoves. He didn't need a microphone or loud speaker because his voice carried strongly and he sang an impressive low bass.

Bro. Tommy was called to the New

Home Free Will Baptist Church in Berryhill, Oklahoma in the 50's. He moved his family of six children and continued in the area of Tulsa, Oklahoma for many years. He also pastored Airport FWB Church, Cincinatti FWB Church, two FWB churches in Claremore. He began the church in Owasso FWB and was it's second pastor.

From Oklahoma he went to the Shawnee Mission FWB Church in Kansas City, Kansas. From there he went to California to pastor the Modesto FWB Church.

He was called to help struggling churches and with his wife, Marie, by his side with her great alto voice and gift for hospitality and evangelism, they left churches with increased attendance and sometimes with a remodeled church and church parsonage. A contractor by trade, he built churches, parsonages, dormitories, altars, benches and whole neighborhoods. Being his own boss, he took time off for all district and state and national meetings. He served on boards in whatever state they were in and he loved his denomination.

The couple supported FWB Christian education, whether it was in Nashville, Oklahoma or California. He enjoyed helping in camp ministries and improving camp ground properties.He was a great supporter of his local communities. Missions was a part of his message. "Either you go or you send," he preached. Missionaries, foreign and home, were always in their home and were supported by them.

He wore many hats throughout his life and ministry and has left his legacy. From his talent as a skilled workman, eight of his offspring have gone into the profession of construction or engineering. As a community spirit, eleven teachers from his family have participated in the public school and colleges. Others serve in the field of medicine, government, law enforcement, banking, chemistry, photography, transportation, business, and many other trades. As a man of God, thirty-three of his offspring have served in the ministry as preachers, deacons, youth ministers, gospel singers, and missionaries.

Nathaniel Burlington Sala
Birth:
Jun. 26, 1856
Indiana
Death:
Apr. 30, 1938
Fairland
Ottawa County
Oklahoma
Burial:
Hickory Grove Cemetery
Grove
Delaware County,Oklahoma

Salina's death he married Mary A. Brown on February 20, 1921 in Granby, Newton Co., MO., they had no children. After Mary's death he married Rosetta E. Bly on February 1930 in Webb City, Jasper Co., MO., they also had no children.

He was an early minister in the Freewill Baptist church in MO, as old minutes state he preached in 1915 in Barton Co. at a state meeting. Nathaniel was married 5 times. He first married Delilah A. Milton in 1876, in Newton Co., Missouri. They had 3 children; Martha J.(Depriest) 1877-1899, Joseph William 1878-1963, and Samuel Edwin 1879-1963.Nathaniel, Delila, and their 3 children are listed in the 1880 Federal Census in Granby Township, Newton Co., MO. After Delilah's death, Nathaniel married Virginia M. Brazeal on October 7, 1882 in Neosho, Newton Co., MO. They had 2 children; Elmer Roy 1884-1928, and Effie Mae (Haworth) 1886-1944.After Virginia's death, Nathaniel married Salina E. Gallemore on July 22, 1888 in Coy, Newton Co., MO. They had 3 children; Minnie Margaret (Crosby) 1890-1947, Clarence Franklin 1893-1957,and Mamie Emaline (Darr) 1895-1986.After

J W Strawn
Birth:
Jul. 24, 1823
Hawkins County, Tennessee
Death:
Oct. 1, 1904
Beckham County, Oklahoma
Burial:
Ural Cemetery
Beckham County, Oklahoma

He was the son of John Strawn, of Tenn. He was married to Mary A. Jennings in 1847, and experienced religion two years later. He received license in 1881, ordination in 1883, from a council of Free Will Baptists from the Row Valley Q.M. Kansas, and had pastoral charge of the Bethsaida church.

Carl David Shivers
Birth:
Sep. 14, 1925
Death:
Mar. 23, 2009
Burial:
Little Cemetery,
Little,
Seminole County, Oklahoma

Carl served in the infantry of the U. S. Army during World War II from 1943-1946, achieving the rank of one of the youngest first sergeants. While in Germany he received many medals and commendations, including two bronze service stars.

God called him into the ministry in August 1948 to preach the word of God for the Free Will Baptist denomination. Since that time he has pastored twelve churches which included: Paden, Vanzant, Prague, Sante Fe, Calvin, Stratford, Springhill, Gaar Corner, Mustang, campground, Cedar Grove, and Memorial of Sulphur. Helped organize and start three churches, Prague, Okemah, and Stroud. He has enjoyed preaching for Free Will Baptists and was a staunch believer in the Bible. Along with pastoring and preaching he was a farmer, rancher, oil field pumper, auctioneer, and real estate salesman. The ministry was always first in his life.

Camey Alexander Sledge
Birth:
May 16, 1870
Toccopola,
Pontotoc County, Mississippi
Death:
Feb. 5, 1951
Valliant
McCurtain County, Oklahoma
Burial:
Felker
Free Will Baptist Church Cemetery
Felker,
McCurtain County, Oklahoma

Rev. C.A. Sledge's parents were Lemuel M. and Nancy Jane Terry Sledge, of Pontotoc Co. MS. On Sept. 14, 1892, in Pontotoc Co. MS, he married Miss Mary Susan DAVIS. It is unknown at this time when and where he was ordained a Free Will Baptist minister. They have an infant, born and died July 18, 1893, bur. MS, so it is easily assumed they came after this date but before 1904. They were found living in eastern Oklahoma, then Indian Territory. His name is in old church records showing that in 1904, he helped Rev. McGee form the Territorial Association of Free Will Baptists, to which Rev. Sledge belonged. This Association of early churches grew rapidly in the early 1900's, so that it was divided to further the progress; one was East Territorial and West Territorial, finally becoming Grand River. Rev. and Mrs. Sledge were early pioneers in all this work.

We must not demean life by standing in awe of death.

Ira W Smithey
Birth:
Oct. 22, 1896
Death:
Aug. 2, 1971
Burial:
Green Hill Cemetery, Davis, Murray County, Oklahoma, Plot: Griffin Section, Block North 5

Rev. Ira Smithey was the son of a pioneer Oklahoma preacher, Rev. J. W. Smithey. Ira worked bi-vocational, and while doing so, organized a church in Oklahoma City.

James William Smithey
Birth:
Jan. 9, 1865
Death:
May 15, 1944
Sulphur,
Murray County, Oklahoma
Burial:
Green Hill Cemetery, Davis, Murray County, Oklahoma, Plot: Old South, S5, row 14

Elder Smithey was ordained at Boyd schoolhouse near Bonham, TX. He came to Chickasaw Nation Territory in the early part of his ministry and began immediately to do evangelistic work throughout the old Chickasaw Nation and portions of the old Oklahoma Territory. In the 1915 Center Ass'n minutes, his name appears as having been elected to bring a message. We have no record of the number of conversions in his ministry nor the number of churches that he organized. We know that he was constantly engaged in evangelization of the old Chickasaw Nation and that a number of churches were organized as the direct result of his labors. Eld. Smithey possessed great power as an evangelist and his method of reasoning on the FWB doctrine was that he convinced ministers of other denominations to take membership in the church. He was a good organizer and did the more prominent work in the organization of the Oklahoma Association. His son, Ira J. Smithey, was also a minister.

Elder Aaron W Solomon
Birth:
Nov. 23, 1844
Death:
Jan. 6, 1920
Burial:
Lightning Ridge Cemetery, Roff, Pontotoc County, Oklahoma
Aaron W. Solomon, was an ordained active minister of the Free Will Baptist church before statehood and after until his death.

Rev L E Staggs, Jr
Birth:
1921
Death:
1962
Burial:
Resthaven Gardens Cemetery
Oklahoma City
Cleveland County, Oklahoma
Plot: Sec. 11
Garden of North Chapel
Minister/pastor to several churches in Oklahoma. Had sons who were also minister.

James T. Staight
Birth:
1875
Death:
1917
Burial:
Dewey Cemetery
Dewey
Washington County
Oklahoma

His name is listed as a minister in 1915 in Missouri State FWB meeting.
Spanish-American War Veteran.

1900 Post Returns Presidio of San Francisco, National Archives Corpl Company A 37th Regiment U.S. Infantry

Harry E Staires
Birth:
Jun. 19, 1904
Thayer,
Oregon County, Missouri
Death:
Sep. 30, 1985
Drumright,
Creek County, Oklahoma
Burial:
Drumright North Cemetery,
Drumright,
Creek County, Oklahoma

The Rev. Staires served as pastor of the Drumright Church a total of 21 years, serving for the first time in the 1930s during which time the church had a membership of over 400. He organized 12 new churches in Oklahoma including the Oilton Church, where he served as pastor, resigning in 1952. He assisted in organizing 25 other churches. Active in the Free Will Baptist administration, he served on the National Home Mission Board for 25 years, serving six of those years as chairman of the board. He was a moderator of the Oklahoma Association eight years and served six years on the Oklahoma Executive Board. In addition to Drumright and Oilton, he pastored churches in Tulsa, Duncan, Oklahoma City, Blackwell and Okmulgee.

Elmer F Steelman
Birth:
1918
Death:
1985
Burial:
Laflin Creek Cemetery, Alex,
Grady County, Oklahoma

Jessey D. Stepp
Birth:
Jun. 10, 1915
Death:
Sep. 30, 1994
Burial:
Bixby Cemetery, Bixby,
Tulsa County, Oklahoma

An ordained Free Will Baptist minister who pastored Bixby and other area churches for several years.

Albert Roma Stewart
Birth:
Oct. 16, 1927
Arkansas
Death:
Apr. 6, 1983
Burial:
Non Cemetery,
Non, Hughes County, Oklahoma

An ordained Free Will Baptist minister who first pastored in California and then in several churches in Oklahoma. He was a veteran of the Korean War.

J. B. Stone
Birth:
Feb. 6, 1878
Heber Springs, Cleburne County, Arkansas
Death:
Mar. 13, 1934
Ada, Pontotoc County, Oklahoma
Burial:
Egypt Cemetery,
Ada, Pontotoc County, Oklahoma

Moved to Oklahoma and settled in Pontotoc County where he farmed and preached. He and his wife were long-time members of the Free Will Baptist Church.

James Gilbert Stone
Birth:
Jun. 16, 1875
Death:
Aug. 4, 1952
Burial:
Lightning Ridge Cemetery,
Ruff, Pontotoc County,
Oklahoma

I knew a man who once said, "Death smiles at us all; all a man can do is smile back."

Rev Luther D Stonecipher
Birth:
May 29, 1917
Garvin County
Oklahoma, USA
Death:
Oct. 10, 1992
Stratford
Garvin County
Oklahoma
Burial:
McGee Cemetery
Stratford
Garvin County
Oklahoma

Free Will Baptist minister in the Ada, Pontotoc Co. OK area.

Edward S. Sunday
Birth:
Jan. 1, 1912
Oklahoma
Death:
Mar. 7, 1966
Guymon,
Texas County, Oklahoma
Burial:
Stigler Cemetery,
Stigler, Haskell County, Oklahoma

His family was from the Cherokee Nation area of the Indian Territory. He was educated at Tahlequah and University of Tulsa, where he received a B.A. Degree. He was ordained a Free Will Baptist minister, and pastored churches in eastern Oklahoma at Checotah, Stigler, and others.

During early 1950's, he pastored at Healdton and Guymon, Oklahoma, where he died, from cancer. Rev. Sunday was a Cherokee Indian, and made his family proud. He was a soft-spoken person, and a very articulate and informed speaker. He was elected moderator of almost every association of churches where he pastored because he was a good parliamentarian and could move business along smoothly.

W. Bailey Thompson
Birth:
Nov. 7, 1931
Lexington, Oklahoma
Death:
Aug. 23, 2008
Burial:
Oakland Cemetery
Poteau,
Le Flore County, Oklahoma

He was born to the late Wooson and Trula (Johnson) Thompson. Rev. Thompson was called to preach at the age of 16 years and happily answered God's call on March 2, 1950. Rev. Thompson married Barbara Jean (Hickson) Thomspon. They welcomed to their lives, Jerry, Bob and Von Thompson. Rev. Thompson began pastoring the Freewill Baptist Church in Poteau, Oklahoma. He conducted over 350 revivals and served as Dean of Men at the Hillsdale Free Will Baptist College and as a moderator of the states of Oklahoma, Texas, and Arizona. His service was held at the Community Free Will Baptist Church in Pocola, Oklahoma. Rev. Bob Thompson, Rev. Cory Thompson and Rev. Keith Burden officiated the service.

Rev James W Tignor
Birth:
Jan. 4, 1923
Oklahoma
Death:
Jun. 6, 1993
Oklahoma
Burial:
Ego-Coleman Cemetery
Coleman
Johnston County
Oklahoma

Rev. J.W. Tignor's name appeared in the 1962 Minutes of the OK State Association of Free Will Baptist. He was with the Folsom Church then. He was also a veteran of WW II.

Thomas Jefferson Townsend
Birth:
Jul. 4, 1856
Texas
Death:
Jan. 26, 1931
Wetumka,
Hughes County, Oklahoma
Burial:
Wetumka Cemetery,
Wetumka, Hughes County,
Oklahoma, Plot: Block 26

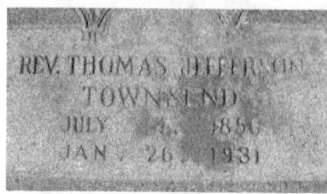

Rev. Townsend was a pioneer in spreading the gospel in the Indian Territory and later after it was called Oklahoma. His name is an honored name in the foundation of the Free Will Baptist work.

Rev Virgil Burl True
Birth:
Nov. 30, 1906
Arkansas
Death:
Sep. 12, 1989
Oklahoma
Burial:
Arlington Memory Gardens
Oklahoma City
Oklahoma County, Oklahoma

He was an ordained minister in the Free Will Baptist church. He and his wife, Wilma, had pastored churches in Arkansas, California and Oklahoma. After his health failed in his older years, he continued to assist his pastor in any way he could. He was faithful to attend district and state meetings of the church.

Melvin J. Tyson
Birth:
Oct. 11, 1932
Ramona
Washington County
Oklahoma
Death:
Dec. 19, 2014
Tulsa
Tulsa County
Oklahoma
Burial:
Morrison Cemetery
Morrison
Noble County
Oklahoma

An ordained Free Will Baptist minister. Faithful in every good work; hard worker, loving husband and father. Pastored and labored in churches for many years, and left a good legacy.

Larry Lee Tuttle
Birth:
Oct. 29, 1946
Broken Arrow
Tulsa County
Oklahoma, USA
Death: Dec. 26, 2015
Sapulpa
Creek County
Oklahoma, USA
Burial:
Prairie Gardens Cemetery
Liberty
Tulsa County
Oklahoma, USA

Larry Lee Tuttle, 69, of Sapulpa went to be with his Heavenly Father after a long and courageous battle with cancer. He was a graduate of Kellyville High School and held a Bachelor's degree from Oklahoma State University. Larry is survived by his wife Patricia (Stout) Tuttle. They met when they were 12 years old at Blue Bell Church and were married on August 13, 1965 at the same church. They celebrated their 50th wedding anniversary this year. Larry was a collector. He collected Briar Horses and Knives. He raised Yorkshire Pigs but raising Bassett Hounds was his favorite. His CB handle echoed that fondness as he was known as the "Long Eared Preacher Man." Larry also enjoyed playing the piano, singing and taking his travel trailer to Natural Falls State Park. Larry was retired from the Oklahoma Turnpike Authority where he worked 23 years.

Larry's true calling was serving the Lord and he did so by ministering for nearly 50 years. Larry served as the Pastor at Pretty Water Freewill Baptist Church for 26 years. Larry loved and cared dearly for his church family.

Funeral services were held at Pretty Water Free Will Baptist Church.

Rev Dale Wayne Underwood
Birth:
Oct. 11, 1932
Vian
Sequoyah County, Oklahoma
Death:
Jan. 3, 2016
Checotah
McIntosh County, Oklahoma
Burial:
Dawson cemetery
Checotah
McIntosh County, Oklahoma

Dale Wayne Underwood, 83-year-old Checotah, Okla., resident, in Checotah. He was born Tuesday, Oct. 11, 1932, to Cecil and Edna (Butler) Underwood in Vian. Dale grew up in Vian, where he attended school, graduated from Spiro High School and received his higher education from Northwestern College. He entered the Army on Thursday, Oct. 13, 1949, at 17, serving for 24 years. He married the love of his life, Nancy Welch and they were united in marriage Sunday, June 1, 1952, in Charleston. He worked full time for the National Guard as a recruiter administrator. Dale taught school in Missouri for four years and also began preaching. He was a Free Will Baptist Minister. Dale pastored in Missouri and Oklahoma more than 50 years. His first full-time position as a pastor was at Greenwood Free Will Baptist Church in Arkansas. He loved fishing, hunting, oil painting, woodworking and vegetable gardening. He was a member of Free Will Baptist Church in Checotah. Rev. Jackie Brown, the Rev. Chris Brown and the Rev. Larry Montgomery officiated.

He was bi-vocational minister pastoring seven churches in Oklahoma.

He was a SGT in the US ARMY serving in Korea. He was also commissioned to serve with the special services missile unit in Washington, D.C. and later served in Germany.

He taught auto body repair at the Tulsa Vo-Tech for 17 years until retiring.

James L Van Winkle

Birth:
Jun. 22, 1928
Death:
Mar. 10, 2000
Stillwater,
Payne County,
Oklahoma
Burial:
Highland Cemeter,
Pawnee,
Pawnee County,
Oklahoma,
Plot: Gate 6 East Section

William Luther Waddle

Birth:
Jun. 5, 1875
Coryell County,
Texas
Death:
Nov. 6, 1956
Cleveland County, Oklahoma
Burial:
Lexington Cemetery
Lexington,
Cleveland County,
Oklahoma

An early FWB preacher. When he was ordained is unknown, but on his WWI Draft Registration on Sept. 1918, he stated his occupation as "minister." His ministry was long, and mostly confined to his home area in McClain and Garvin counties, where he preached and pastored churches with good success. His name appears in old church records as "delegate from Dibble to State Assn., 1935".

Lonnie E. Ward
Birth:
May 14, 1883
Texas
Death:
Apr. 7, 1958
Oklahoma
Burial:
Dibble Cemetery,
Dibble,
McClain County,
Oklahoma,
Plot: Sec 1, Row 7

John H. West
Birth:
Nov. 24, 1901
Missouri
Death:
Apr., 1981
Tulsa,
Tulsa County, Oklahoma
Burial:
Rose Hill Memorial Park,
Tulsa, Tulsa County, Oklahoma

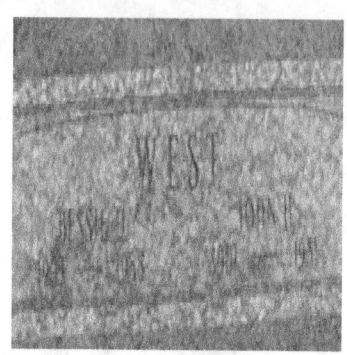

Death Is No More

At first he worked in the oil industry as a pumper. Sometime during this period he entered the ministry, and was ordained a Free Will Baptist minister, date is unknown, but before 1935, for his name appears in the records that year as one of the speakers at the State FWB Ass'n. He entered upon a long pastorate at the First FWB Church, Tulsa, where his ministry was blessed with success. He became known among his brethren as "Mr. Sunday School." His influence extended to young ministers whom he offered training and help to them. He was always active and working towards better education, and was involved in the establishment of the Hillsdale FWB College. The administration building now bears his name. He retired before his death and filled in for pastors and preached at meetings when called upon. He was a member of the national association Sunday school board and very instrumental in its progress.

William R West
Birth:
Apr. 14, 1857
Death:
Oct. 2, 1926
Oklahoma
Burial:
Vista Cemetery, Asher,,
Pottawatomie County,
Oklahoma

A Free Will Baptist minister who preached in the early territory churches.

James O. Williams
Birth:
Jul. 17, 1929
McCurtain, Haskell County, Oklahoma
Death:
Aug. 6, 2012
Muskogee, Muskogee County, Oklahoma
Burial:
Keota Cemetery, Keota, Haskell County, Oklahoma

Bro James, as he was lovingly called, graduated from Keota Oklahoma in 1947 and enlisted in the US Navy in September 1947 and was discharged in 1951 as a Korean War Veteran Radioman reaching the grade of E-5 Petty Officer 2nd class. He spent all 4 years in San Diego, California where he sang with the Melodyaires Quartet for 2 years. He returned to Oklahoma in 1952 and entered Eastern A&M College in Wilburton graduating with an Associate Science degree. While there he organized and sang with a gospel quartet. The Lord called him into the ministry in 1960 and he was ordained as a Free Will Baptist minister in September 1961. Over the next 52 years he preached in churches all over Haskell County, Quinton and the Muskogee First Free Will Baptist Church for 10 years and 13 years at the Porum Free Will Baptist Church. He saw many people converted during his ministry. Next to his preaching, James loved gospel singing, playing the piano for over 60 years. He wrote several gospel songs and was published by Albert Brumley Music Company and Texas Legendary Music Company.

Muril Wilson
Birth:
Jun. 5, 1917
Death:
Oct. 18, 2002
Coalgate, Coal County, Oklahoma
Burial:
Francis Cedar Grove Cemetery, Francis, Pontotoc County, Oklahoma

Ordained Free Will Baptist minister at Happyland Church, who also pastored other Oklahoma churches.

J Reford Wilson
Birth:
Apr. 3, 1924
Death:
Jan. 5, 1995
Burial:
Lexington Cemetery Lexington Cleveland County Oklahoma, Plot: E-R6-10

He was a visionary who pushed Free Will Baptist Foreign Missions in his leadership of 13 years. (1962-1975). The Oklahoma native's ministry spanned 50 years becoming active immediately after his conversion at age 16 in the Spring Hill Free Will Baptist Church in Lexington, Oklahoma. He was the agency's third director and during his tenure the number of adult foreign missionaries increased from 38 to 93. He was an conference speaker, journalist and administrator. He traveled extensively to the mission field to serve a missionary needs, consult the missionaries, attend strategy meetings with field counsels and speak at retreats around the world. In 1965 alone, he toured 13 countries in three months visiting major Free Will Baptist mission fields and doing initial work to open new fields. In 1979, in an article he wrote on world missions, he stated, " No church is properly functioning with real life unless the fire of missions is burning on its altar." He resigned in 1975 and returned to Oklahoma to teach four years Bible and Missions at Hillsdale Free Will Baptist College. In 1979, his final pastorate was at the Butterfield Free Will Baptist Church in Aurora, Illinois where he invested 11 years of his life with that congregation. In 1991, after retiring, he began serving again as Missions professor at Hillsdale College. He pastored six churches in four states: Oklahoma, Tennessee, Arkansas and Michigan. Three times, he was elected to three terms on the Foreign Missions Board. Four times, the Arkansas State Ass'n elected him as their moderator. He also served six years on the Board of Directors with the Evangelical Foreign Missions Association.

He also served as president of the Oklahoma FWB League Convention, conducted weekly radio broadcast as pastor in

Pocahontas, Arkansas, and wrote curriculum for the Sunday School Department. He studied in several educational institutions: Oklahoma State University, Free Will Baptist Bible College, California Christian College, University of Tennessee and Southern Baptist Seminary.

Harry W Withers
Birth:
Unknown
Death:
Jul. 29, 2013
Burial:
Vernon Cemetery
Coweta
Wagoner County, Oklahoma

An Oklahoma Free Will Baptist minister/pastor in the Tulsa area.

Billy Ray Wood
Birth:
Jul. 31, 1928, USA
Death:
May 30, 1989
Pottawatomie County
Oklahoma
Burial:

McGee Cemetery
Stratford
Garvin County
Oklahoma

His name appears in a Minister's list in 1982 Free Will Baptist State Association. At that time he was pastor of Pauls Valley church. He pastored other places also. Son of Louis and Lillie Mae Wood.

He fulfilled righteousness

Frances M Wood
Birth:
Sep. 9, 1909
Arkansas
Death:
Feb. 12, 1996
Oklahoma County, Oklahoma
Burial:
Memorial Park Cemetery,
Ada, Pontotoc County, Oklahoma

He moved with his family to Oklahoma a few years after 1907 statehood. They lived and farmed around Stratford. F.M. was one of the younger of their children, Vard and Walter, also sons. Rev. F.M. was converted in a revival near Stratford, along with his brothers. He entered the ministry in the Free Will Baptist, and pastored churches in the Center Association and surrounding. He also was used as an evangelist. Preachers during these depressed, economic times were more than likely to farm or have other income to care for their family. Rev. F.M. worked some with the Rail Road. He and his wife had one daughter, the late Marie

Wood, who married Rev. James Murray, who is a leader in the church. He was widowed at the time of his death and was living near his daughter, in OKC where he died. He was well-thought of, and was a good preacher.

Weldon V. Wood

Birth:
Nov. 9, 1926
Oklahoma
Death:
Jun., 1967
Burial:
Memorial Park Cemetery, Ada, Pontotoc County, Oklahoma

He was the son of Rev. Vard Wood. He grew up in Pontotoc Co. and was active in church activities from his youth. He married and raised three children, Jan Cason, (dec); Bruce Wood, and Tim Wood, a pastor in CA. He worked hard in the District and State Youth programs, which was called the "League" at that time. He was converted early in life. He was elected as State Clerk of the State Association of FWB, at age 25 yrs, and served for several years until his move to CA. He pastored Ada FWB church, and Capitol Hill in OKC, and probably others before these. He had a big smile, and very likeable personality. He was said to be "a rising star" when he was tragically killed in an auto accident on way from CA to OK, about 41 years of age.

William Vard Wood

Birth:
Mar. 5, 1890
Arkansas
Death:
Apr. 9, 1979
Pontotoc County, Oklahoma
Burial:
Memorial Park Cemetery, Ada, Pontotoc County, Oklahoma

W. Vard Wood, was known in his adult years by the name "Vard". He was the son of James Perry Wood, and Melinda Elizabeth (McBee) Wood, of Arkansas, who moved to OK, early on and died near, or at Stratford. When he was ordained is unknown at this time, but he was converted in a large revival held in the late 1920's or early 1930's and entered the ministry soon afterward, and he served faithfully until his death. He was not college educated, but applied himself in study of the Bible, and other, learning where he found opportunity during those early times. He became one of the leaders in his Oklahoma Free Will Baptist church. He was used often in evangelistic meetings with great success. He was known to lead an exemplary life and his preaching was with power. He had a habit of quoting, verbatim, a verse of scripture, while gesturing as if he was reading it from his hand. His pleasant voice and kind-sounding speech made him immediately affable to meet, and converse with. No known statistics of the number of revivals, converts and baptisms, he had, or the churches he pastored. But he had great success. He was loved and esteemed by all who knew him.

Dr Isaac Wilson Yandell
Birth:
Jul. 16, 1876
Scott County,
Arkansas,
Death:
Dec. 19, 1959
Oklahoma City,
Oklahoma County,
Oklahoma,
Burial:
Lexington Cemetery,
Lexington,
Cleveland County,
Oklahoma,
Plot: SW-R4-41

He entered the gospel ministry at age 16, ordained in 1894, in Scott Co. Arkansas. He moved from Arkansas with his family before 1900, to Indian Territory (Okla.). He

studied medicine at the Vance School in Northwest Arkansas and passed the Federal Medical Examination at McAlester and began helping the settlers with their medical needs. He also farmed as most old-time preachers did as they received hardly any support from churches. He attended the Academy at Kully Chaha, an Indian School the government had set up, and took extended courses at various schools, working at any menial task to support his studies. Kully Chaha debating team would hold debates with the Presbyterian school team at Cameron, where he participated, and acquired a love of polemics. He studied law and parliamentary procedure.

His family moved into LeFlore Co., I.T. where his father died at age 49, and is buried in Royal Oak cemetery of that county.

He preached for the Free Will Baptist Church for 67 years, in Arkansas, Texas, California, and in Oklahoma. He was a leader in the organization of the Oklahoma. State Association of churches and served as its moderator. He served in many positions and offices of the FWB.

He served as president of the Old Southwestern Convention, before 1935, and offered advice and counsel towards forming the National body.

He was active and instrumental in organizing over fifty FWB churches. Many young ministers were under his tutelage.

During his time and era, the ministry demanded many sacrifices from which he did not draw back.

He was a great orator, preacher and debater, and as a speaker was always in demand wherever he went. He never ceased to study, even though he lost his eyesight several years before his death. He could recite many, many scriptures verbatim, and one time after he was blind, he counted 120 hymns of which he knew every stanza. He possessed an unusually keen and retentive mind and wisdom that had to 'be from above.' His wit and humor were enjoyed by all his friends and family alike wherever he went. He lived a life with many hardships, but he always saw a positive side and an uplifting attitude which served him well.

DeArthur Yandell
Birth:
Mar. 22, 1934
Alex, Grady County, Oklahoma
Death:
Sep. 1, 2009
Chickasha,
Grady County, Oklahoma
Burial:
Non Cemetery,
Non, Hughes County, Oklahoma

He was born to Dr. Isaac Wilson and Dovie Lee. DeArthur dedicated his life as a young man to serving the Lord and others with all his heart. He ministered for 58 years. DeArthur pastored churches in Oklahoma and California for many years, and the Chickasha Freewill Baptist from 1999 until he preached his last sermon on Easter Sunday 2009. DeArthur annually attended the Oklahoma State and National Associations of Freewill Baptist Churches, and the State Ministers Conference of Free Will Baptists, where he made many friends.

He was preceded in death by his parents, Dr. Isaac Wilson and Dovie Lee Yandell. He was ordained in the Oklahoma District Association, and pastored Glendale FWB Church for over nine years. He was bi-vocational and preached and "filled in" when asked, after his pastorate. He also labored with his brother, Rev. DeArthur Yandell, in Trinity FWB Church in Oklahoma City. Only a robbery by two gunmen, with guns on him and his wife while made to lie on the floor, caused him to decide to retire from that occupation.

L D Yandell
Birth:
Jan. 5, 1923
Denison, Grayson County, Texas
Death:
Oct. 23, 2009
Oklahoma City, Oklahoma County, Oklahoma
Burial:
Lexington Cemetery, Lexington, Cleveland County, Oklahoma

Strauther P. Yocham
Birth:
Jan. 24, 1909
Death:
Feb. 1, 1972
Burial:
Kellyville City Cemetery
Kellyville
Creek County
Oklahoma

His name appeared in a "Minister's Roll" in 1962 Minutes of State Association of Free Will Baptists, living at Sapulpa, OK, affiliated with Garden Heights church at that time.

Homer Lee Young
Birth:
Feb. 2, 1929
Death:
Oct. 10, 2007
Burial:
Little Cemetery,
Little
Seminole County,
Oklahoma

He was a graduate of Connors State College, Oklahoma Bible College (Hillsdale) Tulsa Univ., where he studied theology. Ordained as a Free Will Baptist minister in 1952. He established and worked as pastor in several churches. First in Henryetta, then to Cushing, Stillwater, Tulsa, OKla. C,ity Moore, McAlester, El Reno, Wilburton, Wewoka, Chickasha. He also served as the Okla. Free Will Baptist State Exec. Sec. He was not only a minister, but a member of the State Minister's Quartet for forty years, which went everywhere singing in conventions, revivals and homecomings.

Buford Francis Zinn
Birth:
Apr. 14, 1919
Porter
Wagoner County
Oklahoma
Death:
May 27, 1999
Sapulpa
Creek County
Oklahoma

Burial:
Green Hill Memorial Gardens
Cemetery
Sapulpa
Creek County
Oklahoma
Plot: Garden of Devotion, 121 D2

Buford lived most of his life in Creek County, Oklahoma. He was retired from Liberty Glass Company. He was a member of Westside Free Will Baptist Church. Although he was an ordained minister, he never pastored a church. Buford liked to fish and visit with friends and family. He and Norma were married for over 50 years.

Everett Eugene Zoellers
Birth:
Nov. 1, 1927
Kansas City,
Jackson County, Missouri
Death:
Jan. 2, 2010
Dallas, Dallas County, Texas
Burial:
Hillcrest Memorial Park,
Ardmore, Carter County,
Oklahoma

Gene and Barbara (Thompson) were wed on November 12, 1945, in Ardmore, Okla. For most of his adulthood Gene was a minister. He pastored at Westside Free Will Baptist Church, Midland, Texas for several years. They then lived and ministered in Dallas.

These two volumes contain over 2600 ministers in 44 states and four foreign countries. An exhaustive work of the ministry of the Free Will Baptist movement; North, South, and unaffiliated conferences and churches. It shares a short biography, tombstone and photo if available.

Volume I: Africa – New Jersey

978-1523824816 Amazon

Volume II: New Mexico - Wisconsin

A Biographical Record of Free Will Baptist Ministers Burial Places

A Novel

This edition has 1217 burial locations covering 44 states and 4 foreign countries from one of the oldest denominations in the United States and covers a vast range of ministers who set the pace for growth and change where they were. In the north this movement were abolitionist and active in the Underground Railroad and began training schools to teach the freeman as they came from the south after the Civil War. They were stronger than the southern group in establishing colleges and active in government. But every territory had its own story to tell. This book will share these messages.

About the Author

Few have walked across the landscape of our denomination and left such indelible footprints as Dr. Alton Loveless. His broad range of experience and multi-faceted ministry has had a profound impact on many lives. He provided capable leadership for one of our national departments at a critical juncture in its history. Even in retirement he continues to encourage others and contribute to the legacy of Free Will Baptists. Thank you, Dr. Loveless, for your faithfulness and commitment to Christ and His church.

Keith Burden
Executive Secretary
National Association of Free Will Baptists, Inc.

FWB Publications

Barcode Area
We will add the barcode for you
Made with Cover Creator

A Biographical Record of Free Will Baptist Ministers Burial Places

A Biographical Record of Free Will Baptist Ministers Burial Places

Dr. Alton E. Loveless

Dr. Alton E. Loveless

VOLUME II

978-1523825844 Amazon

www.ingramcontent.com/pod-product-compliance
Lightning Source LLC
Chambersburg PA
CBHW062049280526
45788CB00003B/1162